25 Keys to a Great Marriage

25 Keys to a Great Marriage

Robert F. Stahmann, Ph.D.
Nathan Wood, Ph.D.

SILVERLEAF
PRESS

We dedicate this book with love and
appreciation to the "keys" to our great marriages,
Kathy Stahmann and Maggie Wood. As husbands,
we are evidence that men tend to marry
above themselves!

Silverleaf Press Books are available exclusively
through Independent Publishers Group.

For details write or telephone
Independent Publishers Group, 814 North Franklin St.
Chicago, IL 60610, (312) 337-0747

Silverleaf Press
8160 South Highland Drive
Sandy, Utah 84093

Printed in Malaysia

Contents

Preface

As marriage counselors and researchers who have met with hundreds of couples over the years, we are constantly impressed with the ability of spouses and couples to be experts in their own marriages. Couples strive to have satisfying and successful marriage and family relationships. They find ways to nurture one another and effectively resolve issues that could break them apart. Every couple goes through cycles of discovering unwanted behaviors and attitudes in their marriage. Fortunately, after making such a discovery, most couples find ways to repair and refresh their marriage themselves. Couples have an almost innate ability to get back on track in the ongoing process of defining and achieving their own great marriage. Our desire is that this book can be one source of ideas and information as you seek to enrich your marriage.

The information we share in this book is rooted in the best scientific knowledge and theory on what makes marriages great. Examples of marital interaction and situations which we describe do not represent specific couples. These examples are combinations of many of the most common problems and marital successes we have seen over the years. You may see yourself in some of the examples. If so we hope that experience can serve as inspiration for you and your spouse as you strengthen your marriage. In this regard, you and your spouse are the experts in what works, or might work, for you individually and as a couple. You two are your own marriage experts. As you read through each of the keys to great marriages which we present, we hope that you will combine your expertise with ours so you can use these keys and have the greatest marriage!

The chapters are not necessarily sequential. You can read them in most any order, though we suggest that you read chapters 1, 2, and 3 first. Read the chapters together, or at lease somewhat concurrently, so that you and your spouse can discuss and apply the ideas jointly.

CHAPTER 1
Using Your Marital GPS

THE KEY: A key to a strong marriage is learning to gain perspective about where you are as a couple so you can successfully navigate your marital journey.

You are aware of Global Positioning Systems (GPS) that can pinpoint your location on land, at sea, or in the air. The most accurate GPS instruments are precise because they use information from three separate satellites in order to determine your current location.

Most couples unconsciously use a "marital GPS system" to navigate their way through marriage. Just like a GPS system, the marital GPS system uses three sources of information to pinpoint a couple's location or marital status. In a marital GPS, these sources comprise information about the spouses and their relationship from 1) past, 2) present, and 3) future. The couple is the instrument that assimilates this information into the marital GPS or, more correctly, a "Marital PPF"—Past, Present and Future.

In the other chapters in this book we focus on your marital present and future. Here we would like to present information about ways that the past, specifically your premarital experiences, can and likely have impacted your marriage. Here we are inviting you to look in your marital "rear view mirror" to gain a perspective on where you've been so you can more precisely map your marital future.

Predictors of Marital Satisfaction

For decades, family researchers have studied what makes marriage work by looking at premarital predictors of marital quality and marital stability. Marital quality is determined by how each spouse perceives the marital relationship and responds to certain questions (for example, questions about satisfaction and happiness). You can assess your marital quality by asking yourself, "During the past week, including today, how happy was I in my marriage?" You could use a scale of 1 to 10, with 10 indicating ecstatic and 1 indicating miserable. All marriages fluctuate in satisfaction and happiness. That is part of life.

Marital stability indicates whether the marriage is intact legally (for example, whether the couple is separated or divorced). You can assess your marital stability by thinking about how committed you are to your marriage, whether you have ever separated as a means to get away from one another, and whether you plan to stay married regardless of the difficulties that might arise.

Dozens of studies have identified four categories that influence the quality and stability of marriage relationships. In this chapter, we explain these categories and list some questions or statements for you and your spouse to discuss in each section. Remember, though, that the research provides a look at what makes marriage work for the average couple. Statistics have been gathered from thousands of couples. However, many happy marriages do not fit into the average picture, and that is wonderful. Since we don't have the privilege of sitting down with you in our office, we don't know where you fit. So, we will present the average picture for you, and you get to use your marital expertise to determine where you fit!

As you read the information and discuss the statements and questions, ask yourselves if these findings are consistent with your marriage. Do these findings make sense in your case? If these conclusions do not seem to apply to you, discuss together why not and discuss how you have used your uniqueness to enrich your marriage. Also consider how these factors might influence your activities as a champion for marriage, which we'll discuss at the end of the chapter.

Birds of a Feather

The first category, premarital homogeny, states that the greater the premarital homogeneity, or similarity of backgrounds and values of the partners, the higher the marital quality will be. Similarities in the following areas are predictors of marital success:

- *Socioeconomic background.* Partners' families of origin have comparable income. This tends to unite spouses in their marital goals and expectations, as well as in their perception and use of money and material possessions.
- *Racial background.* Partners with similar racial backgrounds often share comparable life experiences and familiarity with each other's culture. This simplifies the establishment and achievement of marital goals and expectations.
- *Religious affiliation.* Partners of the same religious denomination usually share beliefs and religious behaviors, which can add a positive dimension and provide a valuable resource for the relationship. Religious behaviors include frequency of

worship with a group or congregation, prayer, and individual and couple spiritual practices.

•*Intelligence level.* Should you have compared I.Q. scores before you married? Not at all! This category relates to similarity in educational level. Both I.Q. and educational level reflect the likelihood that a couple will enjoy the same intellectual activities and pastimes.

•*Age.* Most married couples are approximately the same age. Spouses of greatly differing ages are confronted with more physical problems, such as keeping up with each other, enjoying dissimilar activities, and so on, than couples of similar ages.

Healthy, Wealthy, and Wise

The second category is similarity of personal and emotional premarital resources and life experiences, including the following:

•*Interpersonal skills.* People who have good interpersonal skills will probably use them in any relationship, particularly in one's marriage. Often it is because of these good interpersonal skills that the relationship progressed into marriage!

•*Physical health.* Physical health is an asset anytime. In the early years of marriage, it allows the couple to progress without the constraints and trials of poor physical health. The challenge of poor physical health, for you, your spouse, or both of you, is almost sure to occur later in marriage. Early marital years without the challenge of one spouse being a health caregiver to the other can give the couple a good foundation to deal with health problems when they come later.

•*Emotional health.* Marriage can be a haven for maintaining spouses' emotional health. Every person experiences emotional difficulties such as sadness, depression, discouragement, and anxiousness from time to time. Couples entering marriage with good emotional health have the skills and attitudes to help one another through these difficult times.

•*Self-concept.* A person's positive self-concept (feeling good about oneself, not cockiness or over-confidence) will radiate to the marriage and to others outside the marriage, thus helping the spouses to function well together and in society. You and your spouse can enhance each other's good feelings about yourselves.

•*Educational level.* Studies show that people with a higher education level (schooling beyond high school) not only possess more skills and can earn more money, but also are more adaptable to life's challenges. These people tend to be more tolerant and flexible because their educational experiences have informed them of various issues and events beyond their daily life experiences.

•*Age at first marriage.* In studies done before 1990, this meant that those who married in their early twenties had more stable marriages than those who married in their teens because young marriages were often coerced (teen pregnancy); spouses were emotionally immature; or the couple had few skills in the adult roles required for marriage, including the ability to earn a living wage. More recently, as an increasing number of first marriages occur in people's early to mid-thirties, the findings suggest that more stable marriages result when spouses are older at their first marriage, but not too old. While this is a generalization, older individuals frequently have been on a self-centered road to achievement and **may** not have developed good interpersonal skills. Also, as they have been focused on achieving personal goals, they may not have developed the personal flexibility required for the give-and-take of marriage.

- *Social class.* This parallels socioeconomic background discussed above. Similar social class indicates that spouses have had comparable life experiences, which gives them a shared foundation for developing their own ideas and dreams for their marriage. Similarity of such life experiences as learning to play a musical instrument, playing on an athletic team, and traveling mean that one spouse will not need to convince the other of the value of such experiences for themselves and their children.

- *Degree of acquaintance with each other before marriage.* While many couples know each other quite well as a result of their dating and courtship experiences, many do not know each other very well before the wedding. How have you and your spouse become well acquainted since your wedding? How has this impacted your marriage?

Chip Off the Block

A third category relates to positive parental models. Marital quality and stability are correlated with the following:

- *Parents' marital quality.* Your observations of and experiences living with your parents' behavior powerfully influences your own adult behavior. Thus, if your parents had a happy and stable marriage, you have an excellent model for your own marriage. Discuss with your partner just how this factor relates to your marriage.

• *Level of happiness in childhood.* A happy childhood sets the stage for good emotional health, a positive self-concept, and appropriate parenting choices. With that background, when you become a parent, creating your own happy child(ren) will be somewhat natural.

• *Relationship with parents.* A positive relationship between a child and their parents sets the foundation for positive adult-to-adult relationships. Of course, a few blips in parent-child relationships are normal, so focus on the overall relationship, not the blips. How was your relationship with your parents when you were growing up? How might that impact your relationship with them now?

No Marriage Is an Island

The fourth category involves support from "significant others." Significant others are those who are or have been important or significant to you, besides your sweetheart.

• *Parental approval of the future mate.* Parents are an influence, even in adult children's lives. Approval by parents is important because typically (especially in the early years of your marriage) marriage partners have had an ongoing relationship with their parents and their spouse's parents. Sometimes the parents' support for their child's future mate comes through a process of "convincing" because the mate is not the type of person the parents expected their child to marry. However, we have been told by many couples that even in such instances, the parents now favor the son-in-law or daughter-in-law almost more than their own child! Is this true for your marriage?

• *Compatibility with future in-laws.* You don't marry an individual;

you marry a family. Therefore, it is helpful to like your future in-laws. When we say "in-laws," we generally think of the parents-in-law. However, over your lifetime, you will probably have more interaction with brothers- and sisters-in-law than with parents-in-law. Therefore, you should become acquainted with future sisters- and brothers-in-law as well, and before the wedding. Did you do that? How are those relationships like now?

•*Support of significant friends for the marriage.* Close friends know you. Close friends can give you feedback and information about your relationship with your intended partner. They may have a pretty good idea about whether that person is "good for you" or not by the way you behave compared to your usual self. What did your friends say about you as a couple before your wedding? Were they right?

In addition to the above four categories, researchers and clinicians have identified four other influences on marital quality and stability. These are presented below as statements.

•*The greater the level of conventionality, the higher the marital quality will be.* "Conventionality" describes a traditional marriage, in which roles are defined according to custom. Thus, in the traditional marriage, the husband is the primary breadwinner, and the wife is the homemaker. In such marriages, roles and expectations are clear, understood, and accepted by both spouses, so there is little conflict and a greater possibility for a positive marriage. How does this apply to your "modern marriage?" How clearly have you defined the roles and expectations in your marriage? To what extent have you come to an agreement concerning what each of your roles are? In what ways is your marriage similar to or different from the traditional, or conventional, marriage? How are your marital roles different than your parents'?

•*Couples whose premarital sexual behavior was consistent with their value system will have higher marital quality than couples whose premarital sexual behavior conflicted with their values.* People often feel guilt or shame if their premarital sexual behavior was inconsistent with their values. This can lead to depression or anxiety, as well as feelings of mistrust of oneself or one's spouse. Fortunately, such issues can be successfully resolved by a couple who is committed to each other and to their marriage.

•*Couples experiencing premarital pregnancy will have lower marital quality than couples that did not experience it.* Unexpected premarital pregnancy can be a shock to any couple. The question then becomes what to do because of it. Premarital pregnancy is a crisis, and typically, unmarried, unsuspecting couples are not in a position to deal with such a crisis. Unlike most other crises that couples face, this one does not seem to strengthen marriage; studies show that pregnant couples who marry do not rebound very well from that experience.

•*The more that the motivation to marry is independent of problematic circumstantial factors, the higher the marital quality will be.* Said in another way, if a two people decide to get married because they want to be with each other, they are more likely to be happy in their marriage. This is the most general statement of the bunch, yet it sheds light on the premarital relationship. In many ways, this statement "says it all."▾ What was it about one another that made you want to be with each other? Do you recall any problematic circumstances or pressures prior to your wedding? How have you resolved or overcome those difficulties? What is the glue that has kept you together all this time? Discuss what advice you might give to an unmarried couple facing some of the same concerns or challenges that you faced.

Conclusion

There you have it: a view of some of the events as seen though the rear-view mirror of your psychological marriage. We hope that as you have looked into your rear-view mirror and discussed these things together, you and your sweetheart have also seen things that we did not. You may have been somewhat put at ease by reading this chapter. Others that are struggling may be more concerned about their relationship. Remember, the above premarital attributes are the "average." Just like the "average" American family has 2 children. We haven't met a half a child yet! The point of this chapter is so that you will talk with each other

Finally, we believe that it is a sad condition that the "M word" is on the decline. The "M word" is "Marriage" in the traditional sense of a man and woman, legally wed. Have you noticed that in recent years there has been relatively little media focus on the traditional, monogamous, husband-wife relationship as a healthy and functional form of marriage? Rather, there is emphasis on marriage problems or on other, pseudo-marriage relationships. As a couple who believes in the benefits of your own marriage, you can be marriage champions and help bring the M word back into vogue. When you use your keys to strengthen your marriage, you will strengthen the M word, directly for yourselves and indirectly for others.

CHAPTER 2
Your Love Story

THE KEY: Your love story, which began early in your relationship and continues throughout your marriage, is a key factor in keeping your marriage vital and alive.

What is your love story? On an unconscious level, the foundations for your love story developed when you were young and growing up as you observed husband-and-wife relationships. As we grow older, we develop a "script" about who we are and what our roles *should* be. The script also includes expectations about what we will do in our lives. Our script guides us through our lives. At some point in time we start thinking about love and marriage. As we do so, our expectations become the subtle foundation for our love life—our marriage.

The process of falling in and out of love as a couple began during your dating and courtship, regardless of how many people you dated and how many courtships you had previously. During this time you were beginning to "write" and test what we might term your "joint script," or a couple script. You probably didn't know it then, but this script is what guides your marriage today. Your individual scripts were consciously and unconsciously written and changed (or edited) as you dated. This process continues throughout the years of your marriage.

It was, and is, the defining of your expectations, hopes, plans, and dreams for your marriage. These expectations were refined as you had real-life experiences during dating, courtship, and marriage.

By the time of the wedding ceremony, much of your marital script was in place and had been written, revised, edited, and rewritten time and time again. Our scripts are, in fact, our love story. The scripts include the events—the "what happened" as we dated up until the present. They also include the "*how* events happened" aspects of your story.

As a married couple, you are engaged in a continually changing process in your relationship. This process has to do with how you do things in the moment as a couple, as well as how your relationship changes over time. It has been said that a successful marriage normally passes through the three stages.

Marital Stages

STAGE 1 : The first stage can be seen as the point in time when the emphasis is on mutual *enjoyment*. This is what the honeymoon and months following the honeymoon ideally ought to be—a time when the focus is on the sheer joy of being married to each other. But the honeymoon phase cannot go on forever. As the couple returns to work and various responsibilities, marriage begins to take on a routine of daily living.

As Dr. David Mace pointed out years ago, this need not be upsetting or even disillusioning to the couple. It should be expected. Disillusionment is just "dis-illusion," that is, the shedding of illusions. The fewer illusions the couple have brought into their marriage, the better! But there will always be some illusions. You cannot experience marriage until you are there! Dating, courtship, and engagement are times when illusions of the relationship and upcoming marriage can be discovered and dealt with.

STAGE 2: As a married couple settles down after the honeymoon stage, a second stage begins, a time in which the emphasis is more on mutual *adjustment*. Adjusting to the lifestyle of being married and to your marriage partner requires adaptability and flexibility. This is necessary and inevitable.

Successful marriages take place when a couple has learned the complex dance of how to connect and stay connected with each other in every major aspect of human experience. Connection occurs at psychological, emotional, physical, existential, and spiritual levels of existence. It is true that adjustment continues throughout marriage and should continue as individual and relational needs change. It is also true that couples typically are more aware of their individual adjustment during the early years of marriage.

This adjustment period is a critical process for the success of any marriage. All marriages require that the partners make some adaptation to each other. The husband who expects to remain exactly the same person, doing exactly the same things after his wedding as he did before, just hasn't grasped the significance of being married. The same can be said for the wife. Marriage requires adjustment; the good news is that adjustment leads to individual and marital growth and happiness.

STAGE 3: When adjustments to marriage become more routine, we can say that the marriage passes into a third stage in which the emphasis is on mutual *fulfillment*. This is a quieter time for the relationship. Yet, in many ways it is more satisfying because it goes deeper and is much more enduring than the enjoyment stage.

Thus, you can see the process of your marriage developing after the wedding from a blissful, perhaps even naïve period of initial enjoyment and adjustments which lead to mutual fulfillment. As you think about how these ideas apply to your marriage, you will have another way to look at your love story.

Looking at Your Relationship History

As noted in chapter 1, we believe that it can be an enjoyable and useful journey to travel back in time and look at the history of your love story from its beginnings to the present time. Our goal is that through this more detailed process of discussing how your relationship has grown and developed, you will discover some things about yourself and your partner that you were unaware of and rediscover some things that you have forgotten.

How has your relationship developed and changed over time? Think of your relationship history or love story as traveling along a road. What has been the surface of the road (e.g., paved, gravel, icy)? How have you dealt with the detours and potholes in the road? How have you, individually and together, handled the journey?

Recalling your love story and relationship history should be a shared discussion of your recollections, thoughts, and feelings as you remember them. Expect differences in your recollections. Comparing the different ways in which you remember things can be humorous and insightful. Plan an hour or so to sit down together in a comfortable setting in which you can begin your dialogue about your love story. As you go through this exercise, keep in mind that the goal is to have fun and enjoy each other's company. That is the best environment for you to learn more about yourself, your spouse, and your relationship.

Your Foundation: Before the Wedding

Begin by discussing when you first met. Remember, this should be an easy and fun dialogue between the two of you. The discussion could go on for hours and hours. You may wish to discuss this over several days. Don't be concerned about the time it takes; on the contrary, have fun sharing your recollections and thoughts with each other. Certainly, the questions listed here are only suggestions to guide your discussion. You can and should add your own questions as they come to mind.

FIRST MEETING:

> When did the two of you meet? What year was it?
>
> How old were each of you at the time?
>
> How did you first meet? Did you know who the other one was before you met?
>
> Who introduced you?
>
> What do you remember about that first meeting?

FIRST IMPRESSIONS:

> After you got back from that first meeting (date), if you had a best friend to whom you would have told everything, and she or he had asked you what you thought of the other person, what would you have said?
>
> What did you like about each other?
>
> What attracted you to each other?
>
> What did you discover about each other that was different, unusual, or unexpected?

SECOND DATE:

> How long after the first meeting or date did the second date occur?

Who initiated it?

What were your feelings about seeing each other again?

Where did you go?

How did you decide what you were going to do on the date?

SECOND IMPRESSIONS:

> At the end of the second date, what do you think that your partner found attractive about you?
>
> What did you find attractive or interesting about each other?
>
> Did you discover anything that was unexpected or different than the first date?

EXCLUSIVITY AND INCLUSIVITY:

> Did you continue to date others? Did the two of you discuss dating others?
>
> When did you decide to stop dating others? If you stopped dating others without discussing it, when did you begin to know or sense that the other person was no longer interested in dating other people?
>
> If you discussed and decided not to date other people, how did that discussion go?

FRIENDS' AND FAMILY'S RESPONSES:

> How did your friends respond to you going out with this person?
>
> What did your friends like about him/her?
>
> What did your friends dislike about him/her?
>
> If family members met this person, what were their reactions?
>
> What were your responses to meeting his/her family?

STEADY DATING:

> When did you each see yourself as together, "going steady," or

being a couple?

How did you arrive at this decision?

Did you discuss it or did it just happen?

What did your friends think of your commitment to date exclusively?

What did your parents and siblings think about your decision to date exclusively?

BONDING PROCESS:

When did you say to yourself "She is for me!" or "He is someone I'd marry"? (This can be seen as the point of internal commitment.)

When did you begin to say to your partner "You're for me," or "I could see us getting married?" (This can be seen as the point of external commitment—commitment to your partner, but a secret to others.)

SEPARATIONS:

When the two of you may have been separated for a while (such as summer, work, and so on), what did you say to each other about your relationship?

How do you think your partner saw your relationship?

How would you each describe your relationship as you separated?

What did you do to maintain or cool the relationship during your time you were apart?

ENGAGEMENT:

Did you discuss getting engaged?

When did you discuss getting engaged?

Did you discuss and shop for an engagement/wedding ring?

Was the engagement, or "popping the question," a surprise?

Did you inform your parents (both his and hers) or request their permission/blessing of the coming engagement?

What were your parents and siblings reactions when you became engaged?

How did you see each other's family as reacting to the engagement?

When and how did you tell others, i.e., announce your engagement?

WEDDING PLANNING:

How did your wedding plans develop?

Who was involved in the wedding planning?

What did you learn about yourself, each other, and each other's family during the wedding planning?

How did each of you experience the wedding?

How did you decide about a honeymoon?

YOUR MARRIAGE: AFTER THE WEDDING

Up to this point you have been traveling a somewhat traditional and predictable road to marriage. Hopefully, you have enjoyed and benefited from this recollection of events and the process of forming your marital relationship. Now, lets look at some of the dimensions and processes of marriage itself.

COMMUNICATION:

How would you describe your communication now?

How has your communication changed over the course of your relationship timeline?

How do each of you know if you have said or done something that pleases the other?

How do each of you know if you say or do something that the other doesn't like?

In what ways are you able to express your feelings to each other?

How do you show your partner that you understand him or her?

How do you know that your partner understands you?

CARING AND SUPPORT:

How do you know that your partner cares about you?

In what ways do you show respect for each other?

What does your partner do that makes you feel respected and cherished?

Are there instances that you recall when you feel that you have been taken for granted by your partner?

PERSONALITY ISSUES:

How would you describe your personality?

How would you describe your partner's personality?

Are there aspects of your or your partner's personality that you would like changed?

In what ways are your personalities complimentary?

In what ways are your personalities conflicting?

CONFLICT:

Do either or both of you avoid conflict with one another?

How often do you disagree?

Do you have any arguments?

What issues or concerns have caused arguments?

How did you make sense out of these arguments?

How were the arguments resolved?

Who initiated the making up or peacemaking effort? What was done?

What was your relationship like after you made up?

FAMILY OF ORIGIN:

Do you perceive that any family members have interfered with your relationship? If so, how have you handled that?

Are one or both of you "too involved" with his or her family?

In what way do each of you handle frustrations similarly to your fathers?

In what way do each of you handle frustrations similarly to your mothers?

In what ways do you give and receive affection similar to your fathers?

In what ways do you give and receive affection similar to your mothers?

Which traits of your parents and their marital relationship do you want to carry into you marriage?

Which traits might you like to exclude from you marriage?

What are your impressions of sister and brothers and sisters- and brothers-in-law?

Which family members are you most likely to be closest to as a couple (now and in the future)?

SOCIAL LIFE:

How have the two of you handled your social life during your relationship?

Who was in charge of your social calendar?

Do one or both of you initiate ideas regarding your social life?

Did each of you have friends apart from the other person? Were some friends dropped along the way?

When did the two of you begin to establish friends as a couple that were not known to each of you individually before your relationship?

LEISURE ACTIVITIES:

Do you feel that you have a balance between activities done separately and together?

What sort of struggles have you had over expectations of having a good time?

How do you decide what to do together, and separately, for leisure activities?

Do you share the same sense of what "having fun" means?

Does one pressure the other to enjoy certain activities?

Sometimes spouses feel that mates are either too busy or too inactive. In what ways is this the case for you?

FINANCES:

What have you done to work out a means of handling finances?

Do you share in financial decisions?

Are your spending and saving habits and expectations similar?

INTIMACY:

In what ways do you feel intimate with or close to your spouse?

How do you know that you have a private and trusting relationship?

Are you aware of and responsive to your spouse's feelings and sense of well being?

Couples can be intimate emotionally, physically, spiritually, and cognitively (planning for the future), and in other ways. In what ways do you feel your relationship is intimate?

What areas of intimacy would you like to increase in your relationship?

AFFECTION:

Are the ways that you demonstrate affection to each other in your relationship meeting your needs and expectations?

What are your expectations about affection for your relationship, now and in the future?

How was affection demonstrated in your family of origin?

How do you see the differences between affection and sex?

SEXUALITY:

Is your sex education and knowledge adequate?

Are your individual attitudes about sex sound and healthy?

Have you discussed together sexuality and sexual issues and information to the degree that you feel are appropriate for your relationship?

Discuss with each other the statement "Being sexual is only one way of being affectionate."

Discuss the statement "Sexual relations within marriage are important not only for the purpose of procreation, but also as a means of expressing love and strengthening emotional bonds between husband and wife."

PARENTING:

What are your hopes about being parents?

What aspects of parenting from your childhood do you want for your children?

Will you be, are you, or have you been "good" parents?

RELIGIOUS PRACTICE:

In what ways are your religious values a foundation for your relationship and marriage?

How do you practice your religion in your marriage?

What are your expectations of your spouse regarding religious practice and behavior in your marriage?

What are your expectations and practices regarding such things as participation in and attendance at religious services?

The Glue of Your Love Story

The goal of discussing these questions together and having a dialogue is to show you the "glue" that binds the two of you together. It allows you to write your love story. Such questions can lead you to clarify your expectations—as individuals and as a couple—for your marriage as you edit your marital script in daily living. Hopefully you generated additional questions and discussion on your own, too.

While there are common themes across marriages, it is the unique ways that you generate and co-create your marital script and live your love story that is the key to your happiness and success. We believe that as you have read, thought about, and discussed some of the above questions, you will have a meaningful recollection and understanding of many important aspects of your relationship.

CHAPTER 3

Getting Married and Staying Married

THE KEY: Understanding your reasons for getting married and your beliefs about marriage can influence the course of your marriage.

U nderstanding your reasons, motivations, and current expectations for your marriage can give you insight into yourself and your spouse. It can help you see who you both are and where you want to go from here. This understanding can also be a foundation to build your current relationship on. And it can possibly even give you insights into past conflict and challenges you have faced over the time you've been together.

People typically enter into marriage with a vision of how they will live "happily ever after." Parts of your own "happily ever after" may have some fantasy-like aspects, otherwise known as unrealistic or misplaced expectations. Most of your "happily ever after" expectations are beautiful and should be cherished.

Men and women moving toward a wedding have developed many ideas about what marriage is and what it is supposed to be like. They see in their mind's eye how their spouse will act. They envision how they and their sweetheart will function as married people. People don't get married anticipating unhappiness and divorce. People get married anticipating satisfaction and the fulfillment of their personal "happily ever after."

Many of our expectations, ideas, and dreams about marriage are based upon life experiences; many come from the society in which we live. Some of these imaginings are accurate and some are myths. Countless couples enter into marriage believing false ideas. We have found two false ideas about marriage that can be very detrimental to couples who are hoping to form a lasting marital relationship. The first illusion regards how we meet. The second illusion regards how couples relate to one another in marriage.

Marital Illusions

FIRST ILLUSION: MARRIAGE AND MATE SELECTION ARE A MATTER OF CHANCE.

There is a popular idea that marriage and the process of selecting one's mate is a matter of chance. If the marriage does not work and one or both spouses are unhappy, the fault must lie with bad luck in how the partners got together. You can see the recent mushrooming growth and popularity of online dating and mate selection businesses. These businesses would have us believe that by subscribing to their service and taking an online test, the matter of chance in finding the right marriage partner is greatly reduced and one can be more assured of a good match.

While it is true that you will not know everything about yourself or your mate when you decide to marry, we believe that the process of selecting one's mate is one of the most accurate decision making processes in which we engage. A person chooses exactly the mate they need and want at a certain point in time. Of course, this does not mean that another person could not fulfill some of the same needs as the person selected. It does mean that both partners have chosen a person that reflects their expectations and needs at that time they made that choice. Research shows that people usually know what sort of a person meets their expectations and wishes. People have a remarkable ability to analyze and evaluate these expectations and needs through a conscious and unconscious filtering and screening process, which they apply during the dating and courtship process.

Now, think about this process as it worked for you. What were your expectations about marriage at the time you were married? What criteria, spoken and unspoken, were you judging your spouse against before you were married? How have these expectations changed over time?

If you are having a difficult time talking or writing about these questions, try filling in the blanks of the following questions. Have your sweetheart do the same and, if you're brave, compare your answers. It works best if you fill in the blanks with specific action phrases or behaviors. For example: "A good husband helps with the housework." Another example: "A good wife gives me reasonable time to pursue my hobbies." Try to stay away from general statements like: "A good husband cares about his wife." While caring is important, and everyone will agree that "a good husband cares about his wife," it is too general and may not make your expectations very clear to your mate. How does a good husband show that he cares about his wife? What does the phrase "cares about" mean to you? When filling out the blank, try to answer the question of *how* you know, judging from what is done, that your spouse cares about you?

A GOOD HUSBAND:

(1)_____.

(2)_____.

(3)_____.

(4)_____.

A GOOD WIFE :

(1)_____.

(2)_____.

(3)_____.

(4)_____.

If you want, answer these questions a second time. When you are finished you will have four to eight things you feel a good wife does and four to eight things you feel a good husband does.

Another idea that may help clarify what your expectations are is to think of yourself as a director of a movie with two very confused actors who need to play out your ideal marriage. The actors have no idea about your vision of the ideal marriage, and so you will need to explain to them every little action—including their dialogue—so that they can portray the (your) marriage accurately.

SECOND ILLUSION: MARRIAGE IS A ONE-SIDED RELATIONSHIP.

Society often encourages the idea that marriage is a one-sided relationship. This myth says that marriage is generally uneven and likely to become unfair. Another way of saying this is that in marriage often one spouse will win and the other will lose. This is saying that marriage is an individual experience rather than a team experience.

Couples who come to us for counseling for marital problems exemplify this idea. We find that when people discuss having marital problems or divorcing, the discussion often focuses on the one-sidedness or unevenness of the marriage. Typically, one partner is portrayed as bad and the other as good, one as wrong and the other as right, one as weak and the other as strong, one as dysfunctional and the other as functional.

A couple we'll call John and Sally were typical of the marital cases we see in our clinical work. The way they discussed what the "problem" was in their marriage illustrates this idea of a one-sided relationship. On the outside, they appeared to "have it all." They owned a nice home, were well dressed, and everybody loved being around them. When the couple came to therapy, they said that they had "communication problems." After spending some more time with them, John said, "I work hard and give her control of the money. I buy her whatever she wants. I would much rather be fishing with my kids, but I try to give her everything to make her happy. I love her a great deal. No matter what I do, it never seems to be enough for her."

Sally at this point was almost out of her chair. With a very distinctive look of disbelief, she interrupted, "I don't know what in the world he is talking about! He is constantly at work. He comes home only if I beg to see him. He is a workaholic. He says it is for me and the kids. No way! It is for his ego. He is obsessed. I gave up my life to support him. I still want this marriage to work. I love him. He just loves his job more than me."

Although many marriages may appear on the surface to be one-sided, we believe that couples are usually quite evenly balanced. For example, on the surface one spouse may appear to have a temper, whereas the other appears to be quiet, less assertive, and certainly not angry. Yet, in the private dynamics of that relationship one will often discover that the "quiet" spouse becomes upset and impacts the relationship just as powerfully as the more overtly angry spouse. As the saying goes, often "you get what you give." Thus, while marriage can appear on the surface to be one-sided, with one person losing and the other winning, the spouses, in their own way, are usually balanced. The reality is that in marriage, either both win or both lose.

Motivations for Marriage

Our assumption that marriage is neither accidental nor one-sided has been influenced by relevant research along with experiences in our clinical practice with couples we have seen in premarital, remarital, and marital counseling. It seems that these couples were performing a task and were involved in a decision process when they decided to marry. Many individuals were attempting to fulfill their expectations regarding marriage and their roles in it. They felt that the mate they chose, from the millions of individuals available, was a person who could best provide them with the kind of marital experience they wanted and needed. The search for a mate is not haphazard, but is rather based upon an intuitive "homing device" that propels a person to pursue exactly the kind of spouse they think will fulfill their marital expectations and needs.

Do you recall your individual "homing devices"? The desire to grow and to find a person to meet your marital expectations was likely a powerful force at work during your relationship-building process. This force brought you together.

Although we believe that marriage as an institution makes sense and that the movement toward marriage is in many ways a bid for happiness and well-being, we are aware that the forces that impel people toward each other vary greatly. The truth is that some of the psychological forces at work are positive and others are not. Some of the forces that propel individuals toward marriage can foster positive growth and health, while other forces can bring negativism and sorrow. We want to share with you three of the most problematic and common reasons why people marry.

MYTH #1 : "I WILL BE DIFFERENT AFTER MARRIAGE." OR "THEY WILL BE DIFFERENT AFTER MARRIAGE."

For some individuals marriage promises to be the "great possibility," the solution to the hurts of previous relationships. For them, it will be a new beginning and a new relationship in which they can leave behind a painful past. The expectation is that their new mate will change them and that marriage will in some way bring the caring and loving environment that will resolve their loneliness and hurt. This drive to find a mate who will make one well, whole, or no longer lonely can be a powerful force propelling people toward marriage. This same dynamic can make a person divorce one partner and seek another different marriage that they fantasize will be better.

Now, don't misunderstand us. We do believe that people are different after marriage! The point is that individuals who marry in order to escape or cover up unhappy relationship patterns will likely discover that these preexisting patterns will emerge after the wedding. By the same token, people who marry someone with the hopes of changing them into someone else after the wedding will be sorely disappointed. Therefore, we advocate that during the courtship and premarital time, it is crucial for a couple get to know one another (and themselves) in the many dimensions of marriage. This is discussed in more depth in chapter 5.

Myth #2: "Marriage makes me an adult."

In some ways, marriage is one of life's rule and role changers. There are critical events in the life of an individual and family that bring new rules, new ways of interacting, and new roles to those involved. The birth of a child into the family changes the rules about how husband and wife, now mother and father, relate to each other. Where there was previously the role of spouse, now there is also the role of parent.

The marriage of an adult child can also change the rules and roles concerning how that adult child now relates to his or her parents. Marriage can become a bid for adulthood and a new status within the family. For example, this occurs when parents still try to control and overly influence their adult children's lives, or when young adults have difficulty taking charge of their own lives. Here, knowingly or unknowingly, these adult children may marry in an attempt to change their families' rules. This can be a powerful force impelling people toward marriage if they are attempting to separate themselves from controlling parents.

Myth #3: "Marriage is a way to change the unhealthy dynamics of my family relationships."

The reality that accompanies this myth is that healthy families have an advantage to launch healthy marriages. The other reality is that families that struggle in their interpersonal relationships tend to launch marriages that struggle in similar ways.

It has been said that the family of origin can either help or hinder young people as they try to grow up and take over their own lives.

Some families help people mature, take responsibility, and take charge of their own affairs. In such families, children have begun separating from their parents in appropriate ways as they grow older. For example, these are young people who, after completing high school, go out into the world, live away from their family for a period of time, and develop their own sense of individuality and adequacy. Such individuals have developed the ability to have strong interpersonal relationships and are ready to find a mate with whom they can become both physically and emotionally close. They have appropriate expectation that marriage, based on companionship with one's spouse, will facilitate their relationship as married adults separate from—but still part of—their families of origin.

Another way of saying this is that a healthy family facilitates relationship development so that when children marry they do so because of their belief that marriage will fulfill them. The parents are committed to the idea that their children will leave them, so to speak, and form their own marital relationship with a spouse. In this process, the adult children are able to maintain healthy, committed relationships with both their parents and their spouse.

On the other hand, there can be coercive dynamics in families of origin that drive young people toward marriage because they see marriage as the ticket out of a poor family relationship. Whether the adult child is living at home or not, such coercion to get married can be a strong and wrongful bid for adulthood and independence. Worse yet, the child may recreate the dynamics in their own marriage that they were trying to escape in the first place!

It is not our intention to discourage you if you did get married for any of these reasons. You are not doomed to misery or heartache. We compliment you on your commitment to your spouse and marriage by choosing to stay married! We share these reasons with you in an effort to help you gain understanding. As you come to a greater understanding and accept your reasons for marrying the person you did, you are more free to choose to have a different kind of relationship with your spouse. You will be able to see them, and yourself, in new and exciting ways that you may not have seen before and thereby strengthen your relationship. Remember that spouses working together are a powerful team and can achieve a great marriage in spite of the past.

Marriage Is Intentional and Changing

For most couples in a great marriage, the movement toward getting married is not a casual wandering that brings them surprisingly and unwittingly to marriage. Rather, couples approaching a wedding do so intentionally. They pay attention to their head as well as their heart and hormones. As they get to know each other during dating and courtship, forces build and bind them increasingly together. By the time they reach the wedding, patterns in their relationship have emerged and the framework for their lives together is well established. Most couples are surprised to find how well established those patterns become before marriage.

The following example illustrates how a pattern established during dating and courtship did not reflect the real personalities of the partners. A couple we'll call Jane and Scott were coming to therapy because they were "always arguing about the stupidest stuff." When asked about their dating life, they said it was "fun" and "having fun" was one of the major reasons they decided to marry. They were then asked how they decided what to do on dates and where their dates would be.

Jane said, "Scott would ask me what I wanted to do and I usually said something like, 'whatever you want to do.'"

Scott replied, "At first, I thought it was cool that we had so many similar interests. She said 'whatever you want' so often, I eventually just started planning the dates. She seemed okay with it."

Scott and Jane had established a pattern. Jane would go along with the flow while Scott learned to make most of the decisions. This played out quite naturally, according to their pattern, when Scott planned the honeymoon and selected their first apartment.

However, that pattern started to get them into trouble a couple years down the road when Jane started voicing her preferences more readily. Scott was used to making the decisions and Jane's personal change—being more vocal in expressing her wishes—was throwing him out of his comfort zone. Jane became more and more offended when Scott "didn't consider her opinions or ask for her input."

Over time, as they improved their communication and decision-making skills, Scott learned to ask Jane for her opinion on many things before "making the decision." Jane also learned to give her opinion and feelings more easily. This illustrates the ability of couples to adapt or change appropriately. The ability for a couple to adapt to change is an important skill that helps a marriage grow and strengthen.

Marital Glue and Bonding

In addition to defining marriage as a multidimensional relationship, we would also like to suggest another definition of marriage. Marriage has a unique kind of bonding, almost as if it is held together with a kind of "glue." This glue can be described as the couple's closeness and their ability to have a positive view of their relationship.

Bonding is already at work premaritally, initially tying the couple together. This process continues to bind the relationship together during marriage. We've observed that the bonding process follows a particular progression in most relationships:

- Step 1: The first stage of bonding begins privately in each individual during their dating relationship. At some point in time, each person in the relationship says on the inside, "This person is for me." This bonding process is *individual*.

- Step 2: The next step in the bonding process is *interactional*. At some point after the first step, each person begins to indicate, verbally and nonverbally, that they hold the other person in special regard. This does not take place at one specific point, but is a process. In some sense and in many ways, each person communicates to the other, "You are for me." By this time, the couple is already deep in the bonding process and the relationship has already formed on many important marital dimensions.

- Step 3: As the glue sets more and more firmly, the couple finally makes the last step in the premarital bonding process. As a last declaration, the couple announces to the world what has already happened to them privately and interactionally. This is *social* bonding. When you and your partner (now your spouse) announced your engagement and had your wedding, you declared that the glue was bonding you together. You are getting married because you are committed to one another and to being married. We might also say that you are dedicated to one another and to the idea of having a great marriage—a successful and satisfactory one!

The key in marriage is for the two of you to enhance your marital bond and increase the strength of your marital glue over the years. This is a daily process. If the foundation for that process is commitment and dedication, your marriage will last.

Discuss together how you each see the process of bonding in your premarital and marital relationship. Discuss all the stages: individual bonding, interactional bonding, and social bonding. How have you kept your marital glue intact? What are the strengths of your relationship? How do you show dedication to your marriage to each other?

CHAPTER 4

Seeing Through Rose-Colored Glasses

THE KEY: Couples whose relationships stand the test of time tend to see their partner and their marriage through rose-colored glasses.

Before we show you how to put on your rose-colored glasses, we need to talk about two basic assumptions. The first assumption actually separates what you see—reality—into two parts:

(1) events

(2) the meaning of events

"Reality"

Every second of every day we are surrounded by millions of pieces of information. Our brains categorize all that information, while at the same time enabling us to focus on just a few things rather than a few million. Everything and everyone around us can be called "events." They are events because the world around us is in motion. An interaction that you have with your spouse is an event. Anything that you see, touch, taste, smell, or hear is an event. The most important thing to remember about events is that *events have no inherent meaning of their own.*

The meaning of an event is generated inside your mind. It is an internal experience rather than an external one. We tend to categorize the meaning of events on a continuum with negative meaning on one end and positive on the other. Neutral meanings tend to fall in the middle of the continuum. Attributing meaning to events is very similar to the "spin factor" we frequently see in politics. Let's look at a quick example to help understand this idea of separating events from the meaning of those events.

Hurricane Katrina hit New Orleans in late 2005. As Katrina slammed into the coast and destroyed everything in its wake, many people no longer had homes. Many residents were sent around the country to wait for the water to recede. With television reporting what was happening from moment to moment, the description of what happened was very fact based.

As people were watching the news, those individuals displaced in other geographic locations tended to react to the events quite differently. Some individuals were sad that the hurricane happened, but were nevertheless excited to start "a new life" in their "new home state." They were saying things like, "Katrina gave us a chance we would never have had any other way." While Katrina was certainly a crisis and a painful experience, these individuals put a positive spin, or meaning, on what had happened. Other individuals perceived the event very differently. They were angry that the mayor, governor, and federal government had "let them down." They were miserable and trying to feel better by blaming others for what had happened.

These individuals who responded on opposite extremes of the spectrum could have been neighbors, identical in every way. They only differed in the *meaning* they put on what happened. It is the spin they put on those experiences that made all the difference in their ability to deal with present and future events. This is the difference between events and the meaning of the events. The event plus the meaning we place on the event combine to create what is referred to as perception, or one's interpretation of reality. Let's look at how some individuals seem to live in a half-full kind of world (hopeful) while others are living in a half-empty world (distrustful).

Our Perception Is Our Reality

Take for example what you are seeing on this page. The page you are looking at has a white background with black lettering. Most of you would agree with the previous statement. However, let's change it up some. Here is a brief experiment. As you look at the following words, your job is to say out loud whether the word is in bold, italics, outlined, or capitals.

Bold

ITALICS

Outlined

Capitals

So, how did you do? After a bit of practice you probably were able to complete the exercise correctly and say, "outlined, capitals, bold, italics." You responded in that order because those are the ways the words are printed. They're obvious, right? No, they're not.

Now think about the way we see colors. Grass is green, right? Those of you who have color blindness, what color is the grass? Are you sure that we all are seeing *exactly* the same colors *exactly* the same way? Our perceptions are close enough that we usually come up with the same answer, but there is no guarantee we are actually seeing the same color in the same way.

Our "realities" in this exercise may actually be very different, especially for those of you who struggle with color blindness. Just imagine if we had asked the color of the grass to an individual who was not aware they were color-blind and then tested an artist who sees colors in all their nuances. These individuals would have two unique experiences. Who would be "correct?" Who would be "right?" And if someone was "right" or "correct," would they be able to change anyone's ability to perceive color? Each individual would report what they see according to their reality, to their perception. Our perceptions are distorted to varying degrees by our experiences, previous knowledge, or beliefs.

Adults have years (some of you, decades) worth of experience that has taught you to speak the word written, not the form of the word. All of that learning and experience put you at a major disadvantage on this task. You knew what form each of the words was in, yet you may have spoken the word you saw. All the while, you knew you were making a mistake. The previous training you had in reading out loud acted as a "filter" in how you made sense of the information; it also affected how you communicated the information back.

A common objection we hear to this example is, "But you are talking about capitals, colors, and italics—nothing that really matters." Granted, there are events that have the potential to have profound meaning attached to them, for example, the night of your proposal, your wedding day, the birth of a child, an affair, loss of a job, and so on. But the principles taught in this example do not change. Events still have no meaning in and of themselves, only the meaning you place on them.

Just as you were reading that list of events, many of you probably had different reactions to each one that we listed. Depending on how you are feeling about your relationship right now, the night of your proposal could have been "the worst night of your life," or "wonderful, I wouldn't change a thing."

Filters

We have filters at work in our lives every minute of every day. They affect what parts of events we see, the meaning of those parts, and how we communicate what we've "experienced." There are several kinds of filters:

- Expectations
- Beliefs
- Values

Each of these types of filters has been established as you have lived your life. Past experience has shaped what you think you can expect from yourself, others, relationships, and the future. Those experiences shaped your beliefs and values as well. (Expectations, beliefs, and values are very similar concepts and we will be using these terms interchangeably. So if you see the word *belief* you could also put the word *expectations* or *values* in its place.) The power filters have on our perception can be boiled down to one statement: We tend to find evidence to support what we believe to be true.

You could also say that "We tend to find evidence to support our value systems." Please notice that there are no judgments on our part about whether beliefs, values, and expectations are good or bad, true or false. Beliefs just *are,* and we as people tend to prove them correct, even if the belief is distorted, false, or inaccurate. Horoscopes are a great example of this idea. You December babies out there would be Sagittarius. If you believe in the validity of horoscopes, every time you read something about Sagittarius, you will most likely be amazed on how "accurately it describes you!" You have just found evidence in your life to support your belief.

Taking this closer to home, let's say you have an expectation that "relationships never last." The reality is that relationships go through normal fluctuations over the course of time. Couples will report feeling closer or more distant from each other during these fluctuations. If your filter is that "relationships never last" and you hit the first normal fluctuation of feeling a bit more distant from you partner (e.g., the honeymoon is over), what would you predict your thought pattern would be?

(A) This is a normal transition in a committed relationship.

(B) Things will be better in a month or two.

(C) Something is wrong with the relationship.

The correct answer is "C." It is the thought that will reinforce the filter of "relationships never last." You have found evidence to support your belief!

Expectations, beliefs, and values can open up emotional, psychological, and physical space for yourself, for your partner, and for your relationship. They can also limit your options and freedom in your relationship. The belief "relationships never last" is a good example of a belief that will seriously impair your ability to work through challenges in your marriage. Every relationship hiccup, setback, and bad day will become evidence to prove that your decision to leave the relationship is the "right" one.

We all have filters that will give us and those we love room to move in, as well as filters that will hold us back. The trick becomes how to change the filters that are holding us back.

How to Change Filters (Or Putting on Rose-Colored Glasses)

People go about trying to change their filters in a couple of ways. The first way is that they try to get rid of the unwanted belief first, and then start searching for answers second. This doesn't make any sense! If you succeed in getting rid of the filter that is getting in your way without knowing what you want to replace it with, you are opening yourself up to another filter that can get in your way. An example would be a person that struggles with alcoholism deciding they need to avoid their old drinking buddies. If he doesn't make another plan, then he will end up staying home feeling lonely. It makes much more sense to identify the belief that you *want* to be true or provide another action. As that belief or action becomes more and more a reality, it will naturally push out the unwanted filter. The person struggling with alcohol may choose to find new friends who don't drink and spend time with them. He or she can't be with sober friends and be comfortable drinking at the same time.

A couple we'll call Ben and Janet were in therapy because Ben disclosed an affair to Janet that he had recently ended. Janet was understandably hurt and upset and a very powerful filter had formed. She believed that she "could never trust him again." What made this more difficult was that she had two other very powerful filters that stated, "I love my husband" and "Marriage is worth fighting for."

Ben's filters that created opportunity for growth were similar. His beliefs were "I love my wife" and "I keep my promises." Each of these filters worked powerfully on Ben and were the main reasons he discontinued the affair. He had recently developed a new filter that was getting in the way of repairing his half of the relationship: "I don't deserve her love."

It would be tempting to reinforce both the "I'll never trust him again" and "I don't deserve her love" filters. These beliefs are understandable given the situation. The filters do need to be recognized and validated. However, if Ben and Janet are to move into a strong relationship rather than ending their marriage, they will need to replace these filters.

The best course of action would be for each of them to choose a belief they *want* to be true. A new (long-term) filter for Janet could be "I can trust my husband to be faithful." In the end, this filter will eventually push out the "I'll never trust him" filter. For Ben, he could choose a filter that stated, "I am worthy of being loved."

The following is a list of specific steps that Ben and Janet followed to change the filters that were getting in their way. Each step will be discussed in more detail below.

1 . AWARENESS. REALIZE THAT A SPECIfiC fiLTER HAS GOTTEN IN YOUR WAY.

After Janet felt heard and truly validated and Ben was able to express his fear, they realized that they wanted to keep their marriage. If they chose to keep their old problematic filters, Janet would continue to look for and find reasons why she couldn't trust Ben. And if Janet wasn't in a perfectly happy mood, Ben would assume she was "mad at me" and that she would "never love me again."

2. OWNERSHIP. NO MATTER HOW THE FILTER GOT THERE, IT IS YOURS NOW.

There is a direct relationship between your ability to change and how much responsibility you take for your beliefs, values, thoughts, feelings, and behaviors. As you take more responsibility for what is yours, you gain power over changing it. The more you blame something or someone else, the less likely you will be able to have the life you want. Here is an example of a classic blaming statement, "I'll never be in a healthy relationship because my parents divorced when I was five." This statement has a direct cause and effect relationship implied. The parent's divorce has doomed this individual to a life of relationship misery. The next logical step on this line of thinking would be "My parents need to teach me how to be in a relationship before I can be in a happy marriage."

The person in this example has lost power to grow and change because it was their parent's fault. A statement that reflects an individual taking responsibility for themselves might be, "I saw my parents divorce when I was five, and I have made many of the same mistakes they did in their relationship. I can learn from those mistakes and have a happy marriage." This person doesn't have to wait for anyone else to pursue his or her goals. They have the power to change because they owned their thoughts, feelings, filters, and behaviors.

3. REPLACEMENT. IDENTIFY THE FILTER YOU WANT TO HAVE.

Janet said that she did want to trust again. Ben wanted to feel worthy of love. The reason why these new filters worked so well for this couple is that the beliefs they wanted to have were incompatible with their old beliefs. Another example of this idea would be to replace "I'm an idiot" with "I am smart" or with "It is okay to make mistakes if you learn from them." Below is a list of filters that can limit growth, along with some optional replacement filters.

- Relationships never last. *Replace with:* "Relationships are worth the time" or "Relationships can be fulfilling."
- I'm a failure as a person. *Replace with:* "I have many strengths."
- If I tell my partner what I really think and feel they will leave (or they will be mad, upset, hurt, etc.). *Replace with:* "My spouse wants to know what I really think and feel" or "Our relationship gets stronger when we express and validate each other's feelings."
- I'll never measure up. *Replace with:* "I do many things well" or "I am a good person."
- My spouse will never be happy with me. *Replace with:* "My spouse is concerned about something that has happened. It isn't necessarily about me personally."

People tend to get so caught up in what they don't want that it is sometimes difficult to focus on the replacement of what they *do* want. Take the time to do it! It may be difficult at first, but it will get easier. Remember that you will tend to find evidence to support your beliefs. Why not choose a positive filter so you can find the good in yourself, your spouse, and your life?

4. DESIRE. START LOOKING FOR EVIDENCE TO SUPPORT THE fILTER YOU WANT TO HAVE.

Janet didn't automatically choose to trust Ben right away. Not only would that have been near impossible for most people, it would have been premature. No one expects a plant to grow overnight, and trust is no different. What Janet did do is start to say to herself, "I *want to* be able to trust him." Ben said something similar to himself, "I *want* to feel loved."

All you need to do at this stage is add the word *want* to your desired filter. The next part of this step is more of a challenge. You should start looking for the slightest hint that your desired belief may be true. Janet found that Ben came home when he said he would. Ben reported that Janet touched his arm "like she used to."

This is not the time to expect everything to be different. You are looking for the smallest evidence that your desired belief *might* be true. The danger at this stage is that you will have mountains of evidence for your old belief and only a small anthill to back up your new one. It would be easy to slip back into your old filter. You could call this stage your personal "discomfort zone." The old filter is predictable. It may not be pleasant, but there are no surprises. Be patient and keep going in pursuit of the new filter.

5. HOPE. FIND MORE EVIDENCE TO SUPPORT YOUR NEW FILTER.

This stage is very similar to the last. Replace the word *want* with the word *hope*. For example, instead of saying, "I want to trust him," say "I hope I can trust him." Hope is a very powerful emotion. When we are hoping for something to be true, we tend to gain energy and start looking harder for evidence to confirm our hope.

Remember what it was like to be a kid around Christmastime? Remember the difference between just wanting a toy versus actually hoping it was under the tree? The danger at this stage is the fear of being let down. It would be easier to be let down at the last step and have "no surprise" if you kept your old filter than continuing to hope for your new filter.

At this point you may still have a mountain of evidence to back up your old filter. As time goes on and you don't give in to the fear of being let down, your anthill of evidence for your new belief will grow until it will rival the old mountain. It's just like when you were a kid and started to hold and shake the package under the tree; you started to become more and more hopeful that the present inside was the thing you wanted.

6. ASSURANCE. FIND EVEN MORE EVIDENCE.

At the end of the last step, you were faced with a difficult choice. The evidence supporting either belief was equal. There were two mountains of support: one mountain for your old belief, and one mountain of support for your desired belief. The only thing that will tip the balance of evidence either way will be your *choice*. What do you decide to believe? Once that choice is made, the mountain of evidence that confirms your choice quickly grows into a range of mountains. The mountain of evidence that supports your old belief is still there. It hasn't gone anywhere. It just doesn't seem all that big compared to the range of mountains that exists in support of your new belief.

The only thing that will keep you from being 100 percent sure that your new belief is correct is forgetting how you got here. In other words, you have to keep looking for evidence to support your new belief.

Once Janet and Ben got to this point, Janet's bad moods were just that. Ben reached out to help and didn't take offense. When Ben was out with his buddies, Janet didn't think twice about who he was with and when he would be home. Every once in a while their old filters would sneak up on them. But given the mountain range of evidence to support their freeing filters, the old filters were easily discarded.

7. KNOWLEDGE.

This stage is represented by complete confidence in the validity of your new belief. Actually, it really isn't all that new to you at this point, you've been reinforcing it for a long time. You still need to keep doing what got you here—looking for and finding evidence to support your expectation, belief, and values. Those rose-colored glasses should be feeling really good!

CHAPTER 5
Painting Your Marital Masterpiece

THE KEY: Finding what you have in common is a key to strengthening your marriage.

M arriage means many things to many people. It has been defined in thousands of ways by philosophers, theologians, sociologists, and folklore. Yet, no single definition of marriage seems to do it justice. Perhaps that is because no definition encompasses all of the dimensions of marriage. No matter how thoroughly it is described and defined, marriage has a mystery about it. This mystery may be what keeps one definition from being appropriate for all couples. One size does not fit all.

Couples whose relationships last are able to find their own unique definition of what constitutes a happy marriage. Notice that we used the word "their" rather than "his" or "hers." This is an important distinction to make. A couple's definition is a combination of each partner's ideas of what makes a happy marriage. That combined definition can then become "our" dream and "our" marriage.

In order to find what "our dream" looks like for your relationship, you first need to identify what each of your individual definitions are for your marriage. The more similar your definitions are to each other, the easier it is to create a combined definition. Therefore, we want you to define marriage for yourself and with your spouse.

While each happy marriage is unique, there are many similarities between all of them. We're going to provide a working definition, one that is relationship oriented, but we want you to discuss this and come up with your own definition of your marriage. A marriage is composed of many dimensions. Think of each of these dimensions as its own color. Every painter uses red, yellow, blue, black, and white when they paint a color picture. Yet every picture is unique. We realize that art can be a matter of taste, but the most engaging pictures use all the primary colors and combinations of those colors. We will provide a list of colors—or dimensions—for marriage. The most enriching marriages have each of these dimensions in them.

Your marriage will already have many of these dimensions in it. Or in other words, you may already have these colors in your marital painting. A marital picture is never finished or complete, but at any given moment it is a masterpiece in process. You can develop additional dimensions in your marriage. Read through the following suggested dimensions of marriage and see how they apply to your marriage.

- Social and Companionship
- Psychological
- Cognitive and Planning
- Recreational and Pleasure
- Spatial and Physical Proximity
- Affection and Nurturing
- Sexual and/or Reproductive
- Happiness and Humor

- Spiritual and Philosophical
- Fiscal and Financial
- Legal

Your Multidimensional Marriage

It seems to us that marriage is best defined and described as multidimensional. In other words, marriage is a relationship that functions on many levels. Marriage is especially intricate in its intermingling of these dimensions. The dimensions listed above are some of the most important that we see in marriage. We present this so that you can see the intricacy of your marital relationship.

As you study this list, talk about the dimensions with each other. How would you change what we have said so that your own language explains a particular dimension more appropriately for your particular relationship? How is your relationship similar to each dimension? How is it different in ways that strengthen your bond? These are the *colors* that you have at your disposal in painting your marital masterpiece.

SOCIAL AND COMPANIONSHIP

Marriage has a *social and companionship dimension*, which means a special sharing in interpersonal and social activities. This occurs whether the activities are undertaken together or separately. Often it was this social dimension that first attracted individuals to each other.

However, this dimension sometimes trips up couples later in marriage. A couple we'll call Andy and Courtney met while at a party. The bulk of their dating relationship was spent dancing and having fun with a mutual group of friends. Now that Andy and Courtney have been married for a couple of years, Courtney is upset because they "never go out anymore." Andy says that he is too tired after work to "party all the time."

This couple can do an easy course correction by recognizing that socializing and being around other people was an important ingredient in their courtship and relationship formation. It isn't just "going out" and "partying" for these two. It is the social interaction and energy that helped bring them together, and it can help them stay together. This was an important part of their companionship and enjoyment together initially and apparently an important part of Courtney's marital expectations—a color in their marriage.

A way of increasing the brightness of this dimensional color in your relationship is to find new activities that you can enjoy together. These activities don't have to be expensive. Going on hikes or walks together, bike riding, movies, reading to each other, having friends over, going out to dinner, and so on can be meaningful. You can also take an interest and gain an understanding of one of your partner's hobbies and interests. That way, you can at least have discussions about them.

Here are some questions to ask yourself. If you don't know the answer, you know the person who does. (Hint: Ask your spouse!)

- What are your spouse's interests/hobbies?
- What is it about those interests/hobbies that intrigue them?
- How did they get started in those activities?

Psychological

Marriage has a *psychological dimension*, which means the sharing of emotions and fantasies. Marriage helps individuals reach their best psychological health. The psychological dimension also occurs early in the relationship. Recall how you were "at ease" or "comfortable" in the presence of and conversation with that person who became your spouse?

There are a couple of pivotal things you can do to increase the psychological dimension in your relationship. The ironic part is that you each already know how to do this. You did it when you were dating. Simply be curious about what and how your spouse thinks. Listen to what they talk about. Let them lead the topic and discussion. Asking questions and follow-up questions can open the door to the psychological dimension of your marriage.

One of the mistakes many couples make that will diminish the vibrancy of the psychological dimension is assuming that they "know" their sweetheart. Married people tend to take each other for granted. People change and develop over time. We are in no way stagnant as individuals. To assume you know your spouse will put you and your relationship at a disadvantage. Being open and curious about how your spouse has grown and changed will keep you from "growing apart."

Cognitive and Planning

Marriage has a *cognitive and planning dimension*. This means a special sharing as individuals think about life, make plans, discuss goals, and carve out their futures together. This dimension is closely related to the psychological dimension. It is slightly different because of the focus on the future. While there is an individual component here, the key is planning together for a future together.

How you discuss the future can be influential on your relationship. There can be three ways to talk about and plan for the future. Those three ways are:

1. Your future

2. My future

3. Our future

It is appropriate and beneficial to support your spouse and to ask for support for your individual dreams and goals—the "my" and "your" goals. Be careful to balance those individual goals and dreams with the big picture, that is, the "our" goals.

RECREATIONAL AND PLEASURE

Marriage has a *recreational and pleasure dimension*. This can be another of those dimensions that was one of the reasons a couple got together in the first place. It is closely related to the *social and companionship* dimension. In this dimension of the relationship, the couple enjoys sharing in activities and experiences that form, replenish, and renew their relationship and keep it alive.

Stress is one of the most common factors that is detrimental to emotional and physical health. Recreation and pleasure can actually be good for your individual health, and your relationship health. Just remember to be open to new experiences and options and this dimension can benefit your relationship for the rest of your lives.

SPATIAL AND PHYSICAL PROXIMITY

Marriage has a *spatial and physical proximity dimension*. This means a comfortable sharing of space and physical closeness, and enjoying one another's company and companionship. In this dimension, individuals are comfortable and enjoy being physically close. They feel comfort and trust from this closeness. This is part of their unique "comfort zone" that is for them to share together. You have likely had the experience of another person getting too close to you, violating your personal space, or as we say, "getting in your face." A married person is comfortable in allowing their spouse into their personal space.

Couples with a healthy spatial and physical proximity relationship also have a knack for tolerating those times when one or both "need some alone time." While the overall preference is to be close to your partner, there are times it is appropriate to pursue personal interests, have some down time, or to do things separately.

Affection and Nurturing

Marriage certainly has an *affectionate and nurturing dimension*. This means an intimate sharing of emotional and physical attachment and togetherness that expresses caring, love, and support. It's the ability to express and receive kind and soothing words and behaviors. This affectionate dimension is different from the sexual dimension.

Believe it or not, you and your spouse are not all that different in having a need for affection and nurturing. The main difference between the sexes is how willing they are to talk about it. Husbands can improve in how they talk about the "sensitive" stuff. At the very least, they can try to learn to express feelings to their spouses.

Wives already know the man in their life appreciates affection and nurturing. Wives should not be afraid to directly ask for their husbands to fulfill their affectionate and nurturing needs. Most husbands are adept at responding to specific requests to listen to you or to hold you.

Sexual and/or Reproductive

Marriage has a *sexual and/or reproductive dimension*. This means the unique physical sexual sharing that can be both reproductive and physically bonding for the couple. Unfortunately, sometimes couples immediately rush into a sexual relationship. In doing so, the physical gratification experienced undermines the ability to develop other dimensions of their relationship and may lead them to believe that there's more to the relationship that really exists.

The sexual/reproductive dimension can be thought of as the highlight of your marital masterpiece. All the pieces of a painting are in place and anyone could see what the painting is supposed to be without the highlights. But the highlights add that extra pop, the extra excitement and interest to the masterpiece. The painting wouldn't be the same without it, and yet it isn't the painting in and of itself.

There are highs and lows in every relationship. The sexual/reproductive dimension has a tendency to provide both. Hopefully, it can be the icing on the marital cake. Try not to put too much weight on the sexual highlight; this has a tendency to backfire. Remember that the purpose and goal of sex goes beyond just having children. It is to strengthen, solidify, and renew the bond that holds the two of you together. Yet, the reproductive aspect of bringing children into the marriage, whether biologically or though adoption, has a magic in itself. The marriage relationship takes on a new focus and meaning when the spouses take responsibility for a child in addition to themselves and each other.

HAPPINESS AND HUMOR

Marriage has a *dimension of happiness and humor*, and involves an attitude of fun and enjoyment that develop as a result of the couple's unique experiences together. Marital joy and happiness leads to individual happiness, which has been shown to increase good physical and mental health.

Well-placed humor is one of the best ways to break up negative interactions. The popular sitcoms today typically showcase sarcasm and humor at the expense of another person or one's spouse. This is not the kind of humor that should be used to build a strong marriage. Sarcasm aimed at your spouse can be funny at first, but it can get old and become hurtful very quickly. Left unchecked, sarcasm aimed at a spouse can start to erode all that you have worked so hard to build.

A couple we'll call Spencer and Marissa had been arguing frequently about how and when they would sell their home and buy a new one. The arguments typically took place in their cramped bedroom until one day Spencer said, "I'm tired of fighting in here, let's go argue in the bathroom. I get to sit on the toilet and you get the tub."

Whether or not they actually went into the bathroom, we don't know. The point is that the suggestion broke the tension and the humor zapped much of the negative emotion from the argument. Before we move on to the next dimension, please get the image of you and your spouse arguing in the bathroom out of your head!

Spiritual and Philosophical

Marriage has a *spiritual and philosophical dimension*. This means a specific sharing in regard to spiritual, religious, and/or religious attitudes, behaviors, and life values. What is important here is the sharing and acting upon one's beliefs regardless of what those beliefs are. Many couples report that having a shared belief helps them give meaning to the challenges of life and adds richness to the good times. Research has shown that couples that share in some form of worship and share their faith together tend to have happier marriages, are more likely to have less conflict, are able to reach a mutually satisfying resolution if there is conflict, and more likely to remain committed to each other and the marriage when conflict does occur.

Discussions in this spiritual and philosophical dimension can be very powerful and can help you gain a deep understanding of your spouse. A key mindset going into these discussions is to "make no assumptions." Ask questions to clarify terms used. Ask for examples or personal experiences to help deepen your understanding of your sweetheart.

FISCAL AND FINANCIAL

Marriage has a *fiscal and financial dimension*. This means a particular kind of sharing, not only in the accumulation of money, but also in its use and distribution. The acquisition and disposition of financial and material resources available to a couple have a powerful influence on the dynamics of their marital relationship. Spouse's attitudes are as important here as are behaviors. Often differing views about money and material things trigger feelings of low self-worth, competition, selfishness, neglect, and the like. On the other hand, shared views can lead to feelings of appropriate self-worth, cooperation, selflessness, and respect.

When discussing financial matters, pay particular attention to the meaning and beliefs you have about what money and material things *represent, or symbolize* and the *purpose* of money. Most arguments about finances hinge around differing interpretations of responses to those questions. Find out how you and your spouse feel about money and come to agreements about how you will use and manage your money that you both feel good about. You can read more about "Navigating the Financial Waters" in chapter 9.

LEGAL

Marriage has a *legal dimension* and status. This legal status means that the spouses incorporate their relationship into the civil and legal process of society. The legal dimension also creates a different kind of bond that can keep the couple together. The bond typically takes the form of something like "once married, we don't get divorced." The legal dimension helps create a commitment to the concept of marriage. Combine this form of commitment with a loyalty to your spouse and you have a strong foundation to build a relationship on. On the other hand, if seen as only a legal contract that can be terminated at will, marriage is less of a psychological and emotional commitment and is more easily ended.

Other Dimensions

Of course, there can be other dimensions to marriage. What might they be? Think of your personal definition of marriage or the expectations that you have about your marriage. Ask your spouse about other dimensions they might feel are important. This will help you identify additional dimensions in your marriage.

Now, ask yourself, and discuss together as a couple, what are the dimensions of your marriage? How have these dimensions shown their presence and influenced your marriage during your dating? After your wedding?

Think about this. If marriage is in fact multidimensional—including all or some of the dimensions mentioned above—then during your dating and courtship process, relationship patterns were emerging. You were preparing the canvas and beginning to sketch in the foundation of your marital painting. By the time you reached your wedding, your relationship was already operative on these dimensions, at least in some form. (That is, with the exception of the legal dimension.) The two of you had created more than just a sketch for your marriage. Your marital painting had a lot of color in it.

To say that your marriage began with your wedding is inaccurate. We're suggesting that it is more accurate for you to view your marriage as having begun long before your wedding. As your relationship developed over time and you got to know one another, you were becoming psychologically married. Your painting was well underway. Your wedding announced and legalized that which had already been taking place on a more private plane. *You were psychologically married before your wedding.* Your psychological marriage preceded your legal marriage. This process of psychological marriage continues after the wedding and is the key to keeping your marriage alive and well. You were then and are now painting the masterpiece that is your marriage. Paint on!

CHAPTER 6

Communicating with Your Sweetheart through LUV

THE KEY: Communication is the doorway to understanding, validation, and intimacy.

W e are having communication problems." That is probably the #1 statement couples and families make when coming into therapy. Communication is the crucial piece in marriage. In fact, it's why you married in the first place. Without it, any sense of emotional or physical intimacy is nearly impossible, if not impossible. We don't have to even talk to communicate. A look, a gesture, a smile, or a touch can all communicate volumes of information. What then is communication?

Let's start by talking about what communication is *not*. Communication is not agreement. It is not "being on the same page." Instead, it is the process by which couples can end up on the same page. When you want to reach a resolution, come to an agreement, or end up "on the same page," you are talking about resolving problems and overcoming challenges. Communication is a step in overcoming challenges, but not the end goal of it. Communication can also be used to coerce, manipulate, degrade, and abuse. It also has the power to uplift, motivate, strengthen, and express love. As much as it can bring joy, it can also bring immense pain.

The end goal of communication in marriage is to understand and validate another person—your spouse. It is coming to an understanding of their thoughts, beliefs, hopes, fears, goals, dreams, and desires. The end goal of communication in marriage is connection and intimacy. Intimacy is defined as "a connection between two or more people based on understanding, appreciation, and respect."

If the end goal of communication is intimacy, it must take at least two to communicate effectively. Namely, you must have a speaker and a listener—a giver and receiver—for the possibility of communication to take place. Many marriage books place a lot of their emphasis on *how* to say something. Good speaking skills are important, and can be very helpful. We are surrounded by excellent speakers in society. News anchors, editorialists, and motivational speakers are adept at picking the "right word" for the "right time." Some of our greatest leaders in history have been very good at speaking.

However, in communication the listener actually has more power than the speaker. This is an important point. *Listening draws your sweetheart toward you much more effectively and easily than speaking.* Most people assume that it is the speaker that has the most power and influence in an interaction. Yet, in our personal lives, nearly everyone likes good listeners much more than good speakers. When was the last time you heard a friend come home from a date and say, "It was the best date ever! My date talked about himself the whole time. I think I'm in love!" No, it's listening and trying to understand the other person that is the key to communication during dating. And it will absolutely work in marriage!

No matter what is said or how it is said, it will be of little consequence unless the listener chooses to listen and is able to respond to what has been said. For example, a person may break all the speaking "rules" when they are talking to you, and yet you can correctly interpret the message they are trying to convey. On the other hand, a listener can have the world's greatest orator in front of them and completely miss the intended message. Effective listening requires effort and action. It is by no means a passive process.

Levels of Listening

Effective listening happens at different levels. The deeper the level of listening in marriage, the more likely it is that you are connecting with your sweetheart. The levels of listening can be summed up by saying that you need to LUV your spouse. LUV stands for:

Listen

Understand

Validate

For the sake of illustration, here is a hypothetical situation and dialogue we can use to discuss the details of how to LUV your spouse. Let's say your spouse has been having a difficult time lately at work. Their job is the only source of current family income and money is very tight. At work there are some power struggles between your spouse and their direct administrator. This is not the first time your spouse has come home with an irritable edge to their voice and has been a bit snippy. In fact, you've heard more than your fair share over the past month. As you ask them how their day was, you get the following response:

(Slightly yelling) "I can't believe they put up with that jerk! I have no idea what management is thinking keeping him in that position. I've been running that department for five years and then they chose someone else to promote instead of me?! I have no idea what I am thinking to still work there! I'm going in there tomorrow and quitting!"

How would you normally respond? Would you start to feel the anxiety welling up inside you and say something like, "You better not quit! We need that job to pay for the bills." Or would you just sit there and maybe let out a sigh, shake your head, and roll your eyes? Or maybe you would even sincerely say, "Okay, quit. We'll find the money some other way." None of these options involved Listening, Understanding, or Validating. They involved panicking, controlling, invalidating, and capitulation, but certainly not LUVing.

Let's talk about what the three steps of LUV look like.

LISTEN

The first step in LUVing your spouse is to listen. To listen means that you can regurgitate *what* the other person has said. You were probably a master at this during your teenage years. (Then again, you were probably the perfect teenager and never gave your parents any grief.) Remember when you parroted back to your parents, "I heard what you said. You said . . ." Do you think your parents felt like you "got" what they were trying to tell you after that response? Summarizing the content of the statement is "listening" somewhat. Simply "recording" what someone has said and "playing it back" will not create much of a connection with that person. However, doing so, or doing something like it, can be an important step toward connecting with your partner.

In this example, you could show your spouse that you have listened by saying something like, "They chose someone over you and you want to quit." Your spouse, who is already wound up, would probably respond, "Exactly! I can't handle it anymore."

UNDERSTAND

The next step in LUV is understanding. Understanding another person adds an additional component to just listening to them. Not only are you able to "play back" what they have just said, you can "play back" *why* they said what they did. You are able to perceive the connection between their thoughts, motivations, and actions.

In the example above, you could say something like, "So you want to quit because they passed you up for promotion." This shows that you understand why they are feeling like quitting. This kind of response from you will typically lead to your sweetheart being less defensive. They might then say, "Can you believe that? Five years, I was with them five years and they gave it to the rookie."

Combining *content* with *motivation* in your response is a great way to let your partner know that you are emotionally and psychologically safe for them to talk to. It can soften them up a bit for the next step.

VALIDATE

The last piece of LUVing your spouse is sometimes the most difficult. Up to this point, you have been able to play back *what* they have said, and *why* they said it. It is time to add to the playback an understanding of *how* they said it. *How* someone says what they say is typically connected to their emotions. Many times, simply stating back what emotions are present is sufficient for your sweetheart to feel validated. For example, you could say, "You still seem really angry about all of this." If you want to put the icing on the cake you can add, "I would be mad about that, too." The ever popular, "Who wouldn't be mad at that situation?" can also be helpful. These last two additional pieces of validation can help the speaker feel "normal" and can decrease a sense of isolation in what they're going through. There are very few things more powerful for us as people than knowing that we are not alone, especially to have our sweetheart on our side! Knowing and feeling that is validation in itself.

Given these types of responses, your spouse may say, "You better believe I'm mad. This is just like you said, 'Who wouldn't feel this way.' (Anger at this point is almost gone.) I don't know what we're going to do. I can't quit, because we need the money, but I can hardly stand to stay."

You might continue with validation by saying something like, "You sound like you're trapped."

Your spouse says, "I am. I want to make sure we have enough cash. But, I don't see how I can put up with the rookie much longer."

Now you have a very good idea of what is going on in your spouse's world. They would probably report feeling "validated" if they knew the term to describe how they felt. Notice that there hasn't been a resolution to the problem yet. Feeling validated and valued, which leads to feeling connected, is an invaluable foundation for overcoming challenges or problems that affect one spouse, and thus affect the marriage.

There are a few major attributes and mindsets you need as a listener in order to LUV your sweetheart. They are

- Friendship
- Openness
- Curiosity
- Empathy

- Focus
- Silence

An attitude of *friendship* goes a long way in being able to really LUV your spouse. One key aspect of friendship is that you typically don't try to change your friends' opinions, likes, dislikes, or behaviors. Being a friend doesn't mean you have to agree with what they are saying. Friendship is about acceptance and respect for who someone is, not "who they could be," or their "potential." Friendship gives you the freedom to try to understand where the other person is coming from. You also recognize the fragility of friendship and so you choose your words much more carefully.

Openness is another great attitude to take into marital communication. By being open, you are more likely to learn something new about your spouse and yourself. Humans are always growing and changing. By assuming you "know" what your partner is going to say or do, or putting them in a box, only gets in the way of growth. Being open to new information and knowledge will enable you to keep up with each other—emotionally, psychologically, physically (sexually), and spiritually. Openness combined with curiosity is the one-two punch that can keep you from "growing apart." Being "open" in your marriage will pull you together.

You had *curiosity* when you were first dating. Remember when you never seemed to know enough about this person. You always wanted to know more; it didn't matter what the new information was. The kind of toothbrush they had as a kid was *amazing* information. To rekindle this attribute, try to listen to what your spouse is saying as you did when you were on a first date. You could try questions like:

"Then what happened?"

"What did you do next?"

"What was that like?"

"What were you feeling?"

"When did _____ happen?"

Try not to assume that because they use a certain word or phrase that you automatically know what they are saying. Ask for an example or specifics. Leave the "if they love me they would know what I am talking about" to Hollywood! In real marriages, and in real love, mind reading gets in the way. Curiosity can help with this. For example, if your spouse can ask you to "clean the bathroom," you can—and would be wise to—ask what does "clean" mean to them. You may have thought "clean" was a thorough cleaning complete with bleach and toothbrush when your spouse simply meant a quick spot clean.

The next great attribute and skill in LUVing your spouse is being able to have *empathy*. Empathy is trying to put yourself in another's perceptual shoes. Empathy is similar to sympathy. Sympathy is being able to relate to the other person's experience because you lived through something very similar. Yet, rarely do two people have exactly the same psychological and emotional experience given the same event. Even though you might be able to sympathize, it is better not to assume you know and understand someone else's experience. Empathy will give you insight into how your behavior is perceived. It may not be fun to hear how your partner has been hurt by something you have done or said, but if you listen and have empathy you can learn what behaviors to change.

The final piece of effectively LUVing your sweetheart is to remember that this is about them. Your *focus* is 100 percent on the speaker—on their experience, feelings, and perceptions. This will substantially decrease your defensiveness and increase the likelihood that your partner will feel heard, understood, and validated. Remember, you will get your turn to talk about your feelings, experiences, and perceptions. Now it is their turn.

Before you take your turn and speak, try to sum up the highlights of what your spouse has said to make sure you have heard the most important parts. Briefly summarize or paraphrase. Remember to include the gist of *what* they said, *why* they were responding that way, and *how* they said it (their emotions). Asking if they had anything else to add is also a good idea before you take a turn.

There is one more tip that is extremely useful when communicating with your spouse. It is simple and at the same time difficult to do. It will take practice and patience to conquer this unique ability. The skill is *silence*. When there is a pause in the conversation, just wait. Don't say anything. Don't summarize, reflect, or paraphrase. Don't jump in with a solution. If you can be silent, often times the other person will continue to talk at a deeper level than before. Just when you think you can't stand it anymore, wait five to ten more seconds before you start talking. Don't believe us? Try it out! It is especially effective with kids and co-workers.

Here are a few different communication tips for husbands and wives:

Communication Tips for Him

Tip #1: Understand how the woman you care about tends to talk about an issue or problem. She will not talk to you the way you and your buddies talk. Learn her style of communication.

Tip #2: When your sweetheart starts talking about what So-and-So did at work or what she read that day, your job is to ask more questions about it, to be interested. She is trying to connect with you. If you don't believe us, do a random survey of some women. Just warn your sweetheart that is what you are doing. We don't want the blame for you flirting with others!

Tip #3: When your wife starts talking about a problem she is having, do the following: (1) STOP! Don't say anything! (2) Ask her if she wants advice about how to take care of her problem (that's how guys typically respond to try to help someone out), or if she just wants you to listen (that's most likely how she wants you to respond). Remember, if she is talking to you that means you are very important to her and she wants a relationship with you. If you ignore, interrupt, or give unsolicited advice, you may unintentionally tell you her that you don't care about her or you doubt her capability to solve her own problems.

Tip #4: If your wife is "upset," and there are lots of tears, anger, binge eating, a major shopping trip, or the silent treatment, realize it may not be because you messed up. So don't get defensive and take it all personally! If you want to score *major* points in your relationship, stay in the box. If it does end up being something you said or did (or more likely didn't do), you know that you didn't do it on purpose. She probably knows that you didn't do it on purpose too. Taking it personally when your wife is upset and getting defensive and blaming will just give her another reason to be upset.

Whether it was something you did wrong or something that has nothing to do with you, there are two things you can try:

1. Put your ego in check. Do not be defensive.
2. Ask sincere questions and try to understand where she is coming from. If you do that, you may end up being that knight in

shining armor she thought she married..

Communication Tips for Her

Tip #1: Unless he loves to read self-help books, watch Dr. Phil and Oprah, or has a degree in human relationships, he probably won't be able to read you like you can read him. Most men have grown up with accomplishments and achievement being reinforced. You, like most women, likely grew up having relationships reinforced. These are important differences that affect the way men and women respond to each other. It is an important distinction to know about.

He will tend to be action oriented. Whenever you need something done, he will much more readily step up to the plate. The secret is being *specific* about what you need him to do. If you need him to listen, tell him that up front! If you want advice, tell him you want it. If you want him to clean the TV room and "clean" to you means dust, vacuum, and stack the magazines, then ask him to "Please dust, vacuum, and stack the magazines." After a while you will be able to ask him to "clean the TV room" and be on the same page.

Tip #2: Don't ask him, "Does this make me look fat?" Give him some choices, "Which _____ do you like better?" When he gives his opinion to that kind of question, it will tend to be sincere and honest.

Tip #3: When you would like your husband to do something better or different, make a request of what you would like him to do rather than not do. Put it in the positive. Then thank him for doing it when he has shown the change. For example, if you are tired of him leaving the toilet seat up, you can say, "I really like it when you leave the seat down." Other examples are saying (while touching his arm), "I love it when you just listen to me talk about my day." "I love kissing a freshly shaved face." "You look handsome when you wear

_____."

Tip #4: Most men connect through activities rather than talking. Spend time doing activities with him. Playing computer games, running, hiking, fishing, golf, sports (including watching), and sex all count as activities. Shopping does not.

Now that you have insight into what we mean by LUVing your spouse, you are ready for the next step, that is, overcoming challenges and problems in marriage, which we discuss in chapter 7.

CHAPTER 7
Using the ABCs of Overcoming Challenges

THE KEY: Overcoming the inevitable challenges you
will face is a key to a strong marriage.

Overcoming challenges is perhaps the biggest key in
maintaining a rewarding marital relationship. Think of
married couples you know who have faced significant
challenges. Most often, those couples talk about how the challenges
they faced turned out to be a positive experience for their relationship
later. They say things like, "we are better for having gone through the
job loss." "I would have never learned how strong my sweetheart was
if our daughter had not gotten so sick." The challenges you confront
will undoubtedly stretch you as a couple. Your relationship can be
better and stronger for having gone through them.

It is *how* a couple works through challenges that separate the couples
that are happily married from those who are less than happy. Dr. John
Gottman, a foremost researcher in marriage relationships, found that
there was no difference between happily married couples and couples
headed toward divorce in terms of the number of challenges a couple
faces. The main difference came in how the couples reacted to and
overcame the challenges.

Challenges can be significant, such as a move, job loss, death in the family, or serious illness. Other "challenges" can be completely minor, but they also need to be resolved for the couple to be happy. For example, a very minor potential "challenge" could be deciding where you want to go out to eat on the weekend. The potential challenge comes in the very real possibility that you each want a different kind of meal. Your sweetheart may want to go out for Mexican food while you want to get Chinese. While this is an overly simple example, and it may seem silly to have conflict about this kind of situation, many couples can and do argue about everything from where to squeeze the toothpaste tube to what school their children should attend. The more each person in the marriage has strong beliefs about a given subject, the more of a chance that there will be an argument. Remember, arguments in and of themselves are not bad. It is *how* couples argue that make the difference.

Overcoming Challenges Versus Communication

Let's make a distinction between overcoming challenges and "communication." The goal of communication is to gain an understanding of your sweetheart and vice versa. If you each understand where the other is coming from, you have communicated successfully, whether or not you agree with one another.

When couples come into marital therapy, they almost always say something that indicates they are not communicating effectively. "She doesn't listen to me," and "He doesn't understand me," are all different forms of not communicating. Yet many times each person in the relationship can recite their partner's point of view. According to our definition of communication, they at least have an understanding of each other and have therefore communicated at some level. In that case, what these couples are really saying is, "We don't know how to resolve our differences."

We would suggest that you *do* already know how to resolve your differences. You have done it many times. You just didn't realize that was what you were doing. Each couple has their own way of effectively overcoming differences and challenges.

We have found that most couples follow something like what we call the six steps of ABCs in confronting and resolving challenges. You may use different words to describe each step. How much time you take during each step can also vary. Variations also occur depending on how sensitive the challenge facing the couple is; the more sensitive the challenge, the more deliberate the discussion should be. The following are the ABCs, actually the ABCDEF's, of overcoming challenges.

A—Attitude (Allies Not Enemies)
B—Benefit of the Doubt and Big Picture
C—Considerate Communication
D—Discuss Options
E—Evaluate and Execute
F—Follow-up

A—Attitude (Allies Not Enemies)

Happily married couples have the ability to remember that they are married to someone who loves them no matter what is going on in their lives. However, this is not the easiest thing to remember in the heat of the moment. The secret to remembering that your spouse loves you is shown in how you view where challenges originate. Happy couples see challenges as events coming from *outside* their relationship rather than from inside themselves or from their spouse. That mind-set almost automatically joins a couple together to confront the challenge rather than fight each other. It doesn't matter what the challenge is, be it addiction, anxiety, job loss, or the first child being born.

A couple we'll call John and Sandra came into counseling complaining that they were "growing apart." The situation started out like many of the things that end up challenging a marriage. Good intentions and goals ended up controlling the couple rather than the other way around.

Initially John and Sandra were trying to be supportive of each other's interests and gave each other space to pursue their hobbies. They were trying to walk the road of balancing who they were as individuals with who they were as a couple. John would go out to golf once a month or so. He had golfed with his dad growing up and liked the memories golf brought to him when he played. Sandra liked hanging out with the girls, because as much as she loved John, "he just didn't always get it."

Recently, John had been spending a large amount of time and money playing golf. If he wasn't at the golf course he was reading golf-related magazines or watching golf on television. When he did come home, Sandra would be out with the girls. More often than not, Sandra would have plans on the weekends with her friends. Since she had plans, he would get a tee time. Since he had a tee time she made plans.

When they did talk with each other, Sandra would talk about what So-and-So was doing and everything that was going on with her friends. John would talk about—you guessed it—golf. They both felt hurt and disregarded. John said, "How can she not see how important golf is to me?" Sandra said, "How can he not understand that I need time with my friends?" After all, each of them "were so supportive before. . . ." Conversations were now a threat that required being on one's guard.

John and Sandra worked through this challenge by reminding themselves that their interests were just that—interests. Those activities did not define "who they were." Second, they remembered that they had made it through other challenges together. They made a good team. They were still in this marriage together. They had made it this far.

John was seeing the problem in the marriage as coming from within Sandra. Yet in her mind it was *his addiction* to golf that was destroying their marriage. Her focus was how *his* problem was creating problems in the marriage.

With this awareness in mind, John decided to rephrase how he brought up the challenge that *her friends* were interfering with their marriage. Instead John tried to focus on what his *and* her complaints were, namely friends and golf. He then tried to find a commonality between the complaints. In this case, the commonality for each of the complaints were (1) time away from each other, (2) apparent single-mindedness (selfishness), and (3) activities they both enjoyed.

John approached Sandra, took her hand (something she complained he "never" did anymore) and said, "It seems we don't have as much time together as we used to. I've missed you."

Sandra quickly responded by pulling her hand away and said, "If you weren't spending so much time at the stupid golf course, we could spend more time together."

Remembering that she was not his enemy, he responded (still with some agitation in his voice), "Yes, I have been spending a lot of time golfing lately."

By this statement, Sandra is completely taken off her guard. She is now more open to remembering why she married this guy in the first place. She asks (still some defensiveness present), "If you know you've been spending a lot of time golfing, then why are you doing it?! I don't want to spend all my free time with my friends—I want to be spending it with you. I just never know what your plans are and so I make plans so I'm not home by myself all the time."

John makes another smart move at this point. His mind-set of Sandra being the girl he loves and cares about (aka, ally) enables him to pick out the positive spin of what she just said. John responds, "It's good to hear that you still want to hang out with me. I'm sorry I have hurt you." Now Sandra's defensiveness has almost evaporated and she also apologizes.

This challenge to their marriage is by no means over. They have taken an important first step by remembering that they are not each other's enemy. That, in and of itself, has opened the communication channels more.

So, what can you use from this example?

(1) Remind yourself that your partner loves and cares for you. You are each other's greatest ally. How could we say such a thing? Your partner's anger, avoidance, or silence is most likely because he or she is hurt or afraid. The only reason your spouse is hurt or afraid is because there is a positive connection to you. Your spouse values the relationship they have with you. In other words, they love you. So in a weird and wonderful way, their anger, avoidance, or silence is evidence that they are connected to you and your relationship.

(2) Remind yourself that you still love and care for your partner

(that is why you are probably hurting or scared).

(3) Take a step back and look at the history of your relationship and into the future. Remember that the challenge you are currently facing probably has not always been a challenge. Research and clinical experience shows that most marriages that are currently struggling will be happier in the future.

(4) Verbally express a desire to be with your spouse. This is best done out of the heat of the moment. If your spouse is your ally, what is there to be afraid of? Here are some examples of how to express a desire to be with your spouse positively:

"I've missed you."

"I love you."

"What are you doing this weekend?"

"I'm sorry."

(5) Bring up some positive experiences from your relationship.

"Remember that time when we . . ."

"I remember the first time I saw you . . ."

(6) Talk about the challenge facing your marriage as if it were a "thing" that could sit in your living room. Here are some questions that may help you "put the challenge outside of your marriage."

A. If the challenge were an object or animal (fictional or real), what would it be?

B. What would it look like?

C. What color is it?

D. What is its texture?

E. What is its shape?

When a husband and wife who were battling with a pornography addiction were asked the question, "If the pornography addiction were an object, or animal, what would it be?" The husband, who was trying to avoid pornography, said, "A big, black, lead cannon ball shackled to my ankle." The wife described the pornography addiction as a "saber-toothed tiger covered in oil with fangs dripping in blood." These descriptions enabled the couple to start talking about the challenge facing their marriage in a very different way. They now had a common enemy, the "ball and chain" and the "tiger." When at home, the wife would say something like, "I'm scared the tiger is sneaking up on our relationship again." Sometimes the husband might tell his wife when he is feeling strongly tempted to view pornography and say, "That stupid ball and chain is really heavy today." They were able to start talking about the problem without engaging each other's defensiveness.

To get a better image of how to approach challenges in your marriage as allies, try the following exercise.

(1) Go get a frying pan from your kitchen. Please remember to put your spouse at ease that you are in no way going to use it on them.

(2) Face each other.

(3) Each of you grab on to the handle of the pan with the pan pointing toward the ceiling. One of you use your left hand, the other use your right.

(4) Hold the pan up at eye level, with the arms holding the pan extended. You shouldn't be able to see much of your partner's face. Your other arm can just rest comfortably at your side.

The pan represents the challenge that currently exists in your marriage. For example, it could be sex, money, in-laws, parenting, or how you spend your free time. The important thing to note at this point is that you can't see your partner without seeing the "problem," or challenge.

(5) Keeping your arm strait, take a step toward each other. Doesn't work very well does it? The "challenge" (pan) is keeping you apart as well as blocking your view of each other. This is how most couples describe the effect of their challenges on their marriage.

(6) Now, still keeping your arm strait, take a step toward your partner while turning toward your free hand until the pan is still out in front of you and you are side by side. You now are facing the same direction. You can touch; you can turn your head and see each other clearly, even kiss. The challenge has not gone away, but the two of you now can be united in confronting and working through the challenge.

B—Benefit of the Doubt and Big Picture

There are two "Bs" you can use in overcoming challenges. The first is giving your partner the "Benefit of the Doubt." In the vast majority of marriages people don't hurt the people they love on purpose. Sometimes an individual will take an opposing viewpoint because they like to debate, but they do not intentionally want to hurt their partner. It is important to remember that hurt and disappointment don't go away in marriage, even in happy marriages. Giving each other the benefit of the doubt goes a long way to working through the hurt and disappointment. The ABCs of overcoming challenges work like building a pyramid. The "A" of seeing each other as allies forms the base of the pyramid. It sets the foundation for "B," giving each other the benefit of the doubt.

The other crucial "B" in overcoming challenges is keeping in mind the "Big Picture." It is easy to get caught up in the challenge of the moment and lose perspective. Couples that stand the test of time view current challenges in the context of the big picture. In that view, the current challenge takes its proper size.

To illustrate, take a tube from your paper towel roll and hold it up to one eye while you close your other eye. While holding the tube, stand so that the other end of tube is a few inches away from one of your favorite pictures that you have on your wall. What do you see? You probably see just what the tube allows you to, a very narrow view. The masterpiece may look like a bunch of different colors without much shape or purpose. Couples get into trouble when they assume that the narrow view is the entire picture. Now take the tube away from your eye and look at the picture. You see the narrow portion in context of the whole.

Many challenges marriage face can feel very big and important at the moment. Some of them probably are big and important, like deciding whether or not to take a new job that would require the family to relocate. But that decision is a challenge of the moment, not a picture of your entire marriage. In fact, remembering how far the two of you have come and reviewing where you want to go can be critical information that will help in making your decision. It is like looking through your paper towel roll while backing away until the entire picture is in view. The challenge has not gone away, but it is at least in its proper size.

C—Communication

"A" and "B" are mental exercises that you can use when trying to overcome a challenge. They lay the groundwork for the next level of the pyramid, "Communication." You can review this key to a happy marriage more fully in chapter 6. Just remember, to communicate at your best, LUV your partner. Depending on the complexity of the challenge, simply having an understanding of where your partner is coming from may be sufficient. Many challenges require that action be taken, and communication sets the next level of the pyramid so you can start to work through the next stage of meeting the challenge.

One additional thing to consider when you are trying to communicate to overcome a challenge: Many couples get tripped up on the meaning of words. So it is important to discuss your definition and beliefs about the challenge you are trying to work through. Otherwise you will each labor at working through a challenge only to be left at square one because each of you is working through a different challenge. Perhaps an example will clarify this point.

A couple we'll call Jill and Shayne were seriously thinking about having children. Jill told Shayne, "I think we need to back each other up and use appropriate discipline with our kids." Shayne was excited. He responded, "I'm so glad we are on the same page! I'll back you up 100 percent." (Those of you with children may already see where Jill and Shayne may have a challenge here).

Jill and Shayne had little Allison the next year. When Allison turned three, Jill and Shayne had the first of many "blowouts" when it came to parenting. "I thought you were going to back me up!" was a frequent phrase in their house. The comeback was also frequent, "I will back you up, if you will use appropriate discipline!"

The phrase "the devil is in the details" comes to mind. Jill and Shayne were using the same language at first, "back each other up" and "appropriate discipline." They tripped because they each defined those two phrases very differently. To Shayne, "back each other up" meant Jill would agree with him in front of the children when he disciplined the kids. To Jill, "back each other up" meant that Shayne would enforce what she determined the discipline should be. They also had a big difference in what each defined to be "appropriate" discipline. He believed that a spanking here and there was expected and necessary. She was a fan of the "time-out."

Once Shayne and Jill found out their differences in definition, they went back to the beginning and started to work to find a mutual definition and understanding of what it meant to "back each other up" and what "appropriate discipline" looked like.

D—Discussing the Options

"D" represents "Discussing Options." The business world and inventors have been using this stage of overcoming challenges for years. They just use a different word to describe it. They call it "brainstorming." At this stage of problem solving with your spouse, each of you can grab a piece of paper and for a few minutes write down possible solutions that come to your minds. Do your best not to discount or throw out any idea; now is not the time to judge whether or not it is a good idea or realistic option.

Once you've completed your individual lists, take turns reading off what you came up with. Some of the options will be funny. Others will be absurd. When it came to house chores, one couple came up with "when the house gets out of control, we could just burn it down and move to another one." Brainstorming gets both of you involved in thinking creatively. Many of your options may be very unrealistic.

That's okay. Enjoy working together. Some of the "crazy" options may actually lead the two of you down a path that neither of you considered before.

E—Evaluate and Execute

At this point, you and your spouse are ready to "E"valuate and "E"xecute. We recommend that you pool all of the options from both your lists together so that they become "our" options. This may help those of you who tend to be competitive keep the big picture rather than getting caught up in "my" idea versus "your" idea. Being more concerned about whose idea is chosen will be detrimental to your relationship. You may win, but your relationship will lose.

As you are reading through the ideas you both have generated, you may find that a single idea emerges or a combination of the ideas make a viable option. The goal is for you together to come up with two or three good choices as possible strategies. Then follow these steps:

- Discuss the pros and cons of your possible options.
- Choose one option and commit to try it.
- Plan how you are going to implement your decision.
- Execute your plan.
- Decide how long you will work at your plan. Give yourself days, if not a week or more.

F—Follow-up

The last step of effectively overcoming challenges is to "Follow-up." We have found that this is the step that some couples tend to omit. Don't do that; following up and evaluating your goals is crucial. After two or three weeks (or whatever the time period you determined earlier), sit down and discuss how your plan has been working. If it is working, great! If not, you can make appropriate adjustments. Remember that you have a couple of other options that you can go back and try and then evaluate/execute and follow-up on.

Conclusion

Following the ABCDEFs for every challenge can be time-consuming and a bit redundant. It will even seem awkward. Maybe it is best to try this approach with one challenge facing you and then you can learn and adapt the process to other challenges as they come along. The idea here is for you to adapt these principles to your marital style. Remember that you will want to be more deliberate in following the ABCs if the challenge facing the two of you is more complicated or sensitive. Being deliberate in following each step slows the process down and requires you to step out of yourself and to try to understand your partner and the process of dealing with the challenge. There is safety and positivity in following structure such as the ABCDEF model. Overcoming challenges also helps strengthen your marriage.

CHAPTER 8
Sexual Intimacy in Your Marriage

THE KEY: Understanding each other's ideas about sexuality is crucial to building and maintaining your marriage.

We strongly believe that sex and sexuality is an important part of any marriage. Sexual intimacy is the icing on the cake of marital intimacy. However, it is not the cake itself. Does it make any sense to rate the quality and happiness of marriage by the number and intensity of orgasms when the couple has sex? Doing so would be like saying a house is really valuable and functional because it has three flat-screen televisions. Never mind the termite damage, mold, poor electrical wiring, leaky ceiling, and warped floors. At least you can watch your favorite show in style!

Typically when most of us hear the term *intimacy*, we think of being sexual or sexual intercourse. If a couple says that they have "been intimate," generally the interpretation is that they have had sexual intercourse. This is because of the language that we use and the way that we are generally socialized in our society. However, in your marriage, you are "intimate" in many ways. And most of these expressions of intimacy and closeness are nonsexual. (See chapter 5 on "Painting Your Marital Masterpiece.") Couples can be sexual without having sexual intercourse. In fact, having sexual intercourse is just one way of being sexual.

Taking the analogy above, a cake with all of its ingredients and flavor can represent the many dimensions of marital intimacy. Sexual intimacy is the icing on the cake, and perhaps the decorations on the icing are sexual intercourse itself.

Remember how your relationship became more intimate and personal during the early days of your premarital dating and courtship as you got to know each other? During dating and courtship you developed friendship patterns and behaviors that brought you together and helped your relationship grow. This process served as a foundation for your marriage. Establishing your marital relationship and marital intimacy is a process that began long before your wedding and continues throughout your marriage.

Think of how your marriage is intimate in the following ways:

- How the two of you enjoy doing things together and spend time together is *social intimacy*.
- Your ability to share personal feelings, to trust one another and be trusted, and to feel safe and secure with each other is *emotional intimacy*.
- The way that the two of you share your thoughts about life, discuss goals and plans for the future, and live your marriage is *psychological intimacy*.
- The way that the two of you deal with your decisions concerning how you will earn and spend money and how you manage your other material resources is *financial intimacy*.
- The way that you deal with your families of origin, brothers- and sisters-in-law, and other extended family relationships is

intergenerational intimacy.

- Your unique way of sharing spiritual and religious attitudes, behaviors, and life experiences is *spiritual intimacy.*
- How you display affection and nurture and support each other physically and emotionally in nonsexual ways is *physical intimacy.*
- The way in which you share your love for each other by sharing your bodies and physically become one is *sexual intimacy.*

Regardless of individual's ideas about intimacy, people in marriage are looking for an intimate relationship that has at least four components.

1. First, an intimate marriage is one in which genuine concern for the other person's well-being is paramount. We often say that spouses "care for each other" more than anyone or anything else.
2. Second, there must be mutual trust. That is, the feeling that you will not be harmed or hurt by your spouse.
3. Third, there is recognition by you that your spouse accepts you and approves of you as a person.
4. Fourth, there is a commitment to each other and to the marriage based on the feeling and knowledge that you are dedicated to each other for the long term.

A relationship with these qualities of caring, mutual trust, and acceptance sets the foundation for healthy nonsexual and sexual intimacy in marriage.

While it is certainly possible that a couple can begin a relationship first as a sexual relationship, it is not desirable. This is because often the sheer passion of a sexual relationship gives one a false impression that the relationship may have more psychological and emotional meaning that it has. Also, it is possible that an early sexual relationship engenders feelings of remorse or guilt on the part of one or both partners. We say this not to be judgmental, but simply to point out the emotional and psychological processes that can occur in individuals.

Yet, the sexual relationship in marriage is very important and very much a part of the bonding process. Sex in marriage is closely linked to the emotional aspects of your relationship. We find that in most marriages, couples strive to achieve a sexual relationship that expresses, sustains, and renews their deepest and most tender feelings for each other. Being sexually skilled does not necessarily create true intimacy. On the other hand, real intimacy can create a fulfilling sex life.

Sexual Meaning

Typically, sex and physical affection have different meanings for boys and girls, men and women. These differences, which were learned directly and indirectly throughout our lives, play an important part in our expectations and desires regarding our sexual relationship in marriage. Not only are boys and girls socialized and taught differently about affection and being affectionate, boys and girls are taught differently about dealing with and expressing feelings. In general, girls and women share more easily and naturally than boys and men. They express affection verbally and physically, and give and receive hugs and embraces comfortably. Girls and women express feelings freely; boys and men do not. It has been said that men have a hard time identifying their feelings let alone expressing them! Having said that, we firmly believe that you, as a married couple, have the ability to discuss intimacy and sexuality as it applies to your relationship. After all, you are experts in knowing your feelings and desires, and you have a trusted spouse with whom you can discuss these things confidentially.

There are several areas for couples to discuss regarding their sexual relationship. We suggest that you talk about these questions and use them to guide your discussion. The order in which we present them is not particularly important. Some of these questions deal with your current relationship and others deal with your upbringing and experiences. You will note that some of these questions are framed in a language of *individual* attitudes. Of course, your shared attitudes are also important, yet we want you to consider your individual attitudes as they play themselves out in your marriage. Ask yourselves:

- What are our individual attitudes about sex? What is the purpose of sex? What role would you like sex to play in our relationship?
- Where did you learn about sex? What did you learn about sex? Have you read reliable information about male and female anatomy, sexual arousal and response, sexual functioning, and so on? Married couples seeking out and studying such information together can be very helpful in building a strong sexual relationship.
- Can you discuss openly and together your sexual feelings, desires, and responses? Many couples find it a bit awkward to discuss such things. However, remember that you are in a caring and trusting marriage and part of that intimate relationship is to be able to discuss sexual feelings and behaviors.
- Do you agree on your sexual experiences and behaviors? There should be no coercion of each other by demanding sexual experiences. Those couples that enjoy a positive sexual

relationship work together to decide and discover what is satisfying and comfortable for both of them. Trusting and being sensitive to each other in your sexual experiences enhances nonsexual intimacy in your marriage.

• When being sexual, do you put the emphasis on sex as a loving *experience* and not as a *performance?* Unfortunately, many books, movies, television shows, and public attitudes emphasize performance as the main ingredient for a satisfying sexual relationship. Typically, love, tender caring, and a committed marital relationship are not mentioned. In marriage, an extreme focus on performance can lead to unnecessary sexual anxiety and even sexual dysfunctions.

Sexual Desire

As a married couple, you should anticipate that you will have differences in sexual desire and sexual interest. We're not saying that you will never be interested in sex at the same time, rather we're saying that you will not *always* be interested, particularly to the same degree, at all times. The myth of simultaneous interest in sex is just as erroneous as the myth of always needing to have simultaneous orgasms during sex. Certainly, individual factors such as distractions, physical conditions, fatigue, demands on one's time, and so on can lead to a temporary lack of sexual interest or desire. Even with such conditions operating, it can be said that men and women stereotypically have somewhat different psychological motivations underlying their sexual interest.

For the husband, typically sexual desire is more spontaneous and triggered by his desire for physical sexual satisfaction—that is, an orgasmic release. Because of their physical makeup, men are more easily and quickly sexually aroused than women. For the husband, enhancing emotional closeness with his wife is often a secondary motivation for sexual activity. Consequently, for the husband, physical desire often precedes the desire for emotional intimacy or closeness with his wife. However, it is important to state that emotional intimacy or closeness for the husband follows sexual intercourse and is very important to him. This is evidenced by the fact that many wives report that their husbands "seem nicer" *after* sexual intercourse. Similarly, husbands report positive emotions and feelings following sexual activity, such as feeling emotionally closer and better able to express their feelings.

For the wife, typically sexual desire is more influenced by her desire to be emotionally intimate and close to her husband. This intimacy-based desire motivates her to become physically involved with her husband. During that physical involvement (foreplay) she becomes physiologically and psychologically sexually aroused. Thus, for the wife, her desire for emotional intimacy or closeness often precedes physical arousal or desire. However, physical arousal follows and is very important for her. Again, keep in mind that these are generalizations meant to guide your thinking about your relationship. Of course there are times when both of you will be mutually aroused and desire a sexual experience.

The Sexual Response Cycle

Research on sexual functioning has provided information that lays to rest many myths regarding human sexual arousal and sexual response. Understanding the human sexual response cycle can help a couple to be more aware of what is happening to their own body as well as their spouse's. This awareness can facilitate conversation and understanding which makes sexual time together more relaxing. Researchers and clinicians have identified four specific phases in the human sexual response cycle. The four physiological phases of the sexual response cycle are excitement, plateau, orgasm, and resolution.

PHASE I

The excitement or arousal phase begins when a sensory event or thought stimulates the nerves and hormones. Blood rushes to the pelvic area for both men and women. In the male, the blood causes the penis to become erect. In the female it causes a fluid to be secreted from the internal glands just outside the vagina, as well as from the vaginal walls. The vulva becomes wet. After some 15 seconds to a minute or so, the male becomes fully aroused with an erection. For the female, full arousal of her sexual organs requires considerably more time. During the excitement phase there is a buildup of sexual excitement for both men and women as respiration, heart rate, and blood pressure increases.

PHASE II

The plateau (or foreplay) phase of sexual response follows. The time of this phase varies considerably and begins with full arousal and ends with orgasm. Thus, depending on the situation, the plateau phase may last a few minutes or even exceeding an hour. For the wife to be more fully aroused and enjoy the sexual experience, it is desirable that the couples spend more than just a few minutes—thirty minutes or so is recommended—in foreplay. During this phase, sexual excitement and feelings are at their height.

PHASE III

The orgasm phase is a release of all the built-up sexual excitement in a sudden increase of pleasure. Men ejaculate, and women experience rhythmic contractions of all the muscles involving the pelvic area, which include muscles around both the vagina and vaginal opening.

PHASE IV

The resolution phase follows climax or orgasm. After a man climaxes, a refractory period occurs during which he is unable to become fully erect and climax again. This time is highly variable among men, varying from minutes to hours depending on several factors, including fatigue and age. As a man ages, the refractory period lengthens. Women, on the other hand, can continue to climax and experience subsequent orgasms that may even become progressively stronger than previous ones.

Immediately after orgasm, in both men and women, the blood leaves the pelvic region, all the muscles relax, and a feeling of peace permeates the entire body. Heart rate, blood pressure, and respiration gradually return to normal. In men, a chemical is released in their brain that stimulates sleep. Unfortunately, this same response has not been documented for women!

Potential Frustrations

What are some potential frustrations for a couple's sexual relationship? Of course there can be many, but we have found a few that are worth mentioning. Sadly, one of the most common frustrations is that couples are too busy; they just don't have enough time for their sexual relationship. When we discuss sexuality with couples in counseling, we often find that while they desire and value a good, rewarding sexual relationship, it is a low priority in their lives. We come to this conclusion simply by judging the way they behave. We find that couples often "find time" for their sexual relationship late at night when they are both physically and emotionally exhausted. Somehow they expect their bodies to function as if they were not tired and it was not late at night. Also, often at the end of the day, one spouse or the other will be preoccupied with thoughts or feelings from events that occurred during the day. With such factors operating in their bodies and minds, is it any wonder that the sexual relationship is often hurried, distracted, or unfulfilling?

Other factors that we find which may frustrate or inhibit a couple's sexual relationship include such things as lack of knowledge or information. As we stated above, it is important for you to gain such information. Obtaining this information together can be a strengthening activity for your marriage. Another problem is that sometimes couples, or individuals, feel guilty about being sexual. If this is the case, it is important to discuss it and try to determine the causes for such feelings. Perhaps such feelings are related to one's upbringing or values and attitudes that have been learned along the way. In addition to trying to find the causes and resolve these issues yourselves, there are also resources such as professional or religious counselors that might assist in dealing with these issues.

Sometimes factors such as fear of pregnancy, or conversely the desire to become pregnant, can be related to frustrations and fears that inhibit sexual fulfillment. It is true that the psychological aspects of a person's being are closely intertwined with physical functioning. What can you do?

A satisfying affectionate and sexual relationship is maintained through behaviors and attitudes that show care and love for your spouse. Husbands, continue to learn as much as you can about your wife, just as you did when you were courting her. Remember that little things mean a lot. What are some of those little things that you can do that show her you care for her? Be considerate and thoughtful.

Love her as a person and never criticize her. Believe it or not, personal hygiene is important. Be aware of offensive body orders, your scruffy beard, and so on. Keep clean and well groomed.

What might wives do? First, realize that your husband does not instinctively know what you want physically, sexually, or emotionally. It works wonders sometimes just to tell him what you want or what you like. Certainly don't do this in a demanding or criticizing way, but in ways that you know he will appreciate and understand. Sometimes a wife does not realize that it may be helpful or necessary for her to instruct her husband in the areas of sexuality related to her body. Your grooming is important too. It has been found that typically men are more visual than women, and that undoubtedly is true in marital sexuality.

Protecting Your Sexual Relationship

Your sexual relationship will change throughout your marriage. Other aspects of your marriage relationship will change too. Here are some thoughts that you might consider together as you view strengthening and protecting your sexual relationship.

- Spend time together. The greatest marriage killers are when a spouse cannot give adequate time and attention to their marriage. Are you giving adequate time and attention to your sexual relationship? Discuss this, and determine what is adequate time and attention for you and what you can do about it.
- Have a date night once a week. Getting away, at least weekly, as a couple is something that you should do throughout the years of your marriage.

- Take time for romance. Remember that romance is more than being sexual. Remember how romantic you were during your courtship? Why not have such romantic attitudes and behaviors be a part of your marriage?
- Remember that the being sexual is not limited to having sexual intercourse.
- Realize that learning to be sexual is one of the lifelong goals of your marriage. It's a great joy to share this experience together as husband and wife. Learning to be sexual together is one of the key bonding experiences in marriage.
- Remember that good sex is not just a matter of "pushing the right buttons." Be sensitive to yourselves and each other as you experience a variety of sexual experiences. Don't let sexual interaction become a matter of routine.
- Never carry anger or criticism into the bedroom. The bedroom should be a place to relax and enjoy each other. It should not be a place for arguing and for resolving difficult issues. Serious discussions and problem solving should be done in other places.
- Keep your sexual and other expectations realistic. Don't be overly influenced by what you read, what you hear, or what you see portrayed in movies or the media. Your sexual expectations should be those that are created by and agreed to by you as wife and husband.
- Don't make sex too serious. It should be fun. The sexual aspect of your relationship is a time of renewal and extending your marital intimacy. It is vitally important, yet it is straightforwardly achieved in marriage.
- Finally, don't confuse sex and affection. Be affectionate without

it leading to sex. Unfortunately, we see couples in counseling who have learned to interpret any show of affection as meaning that it is a request for being sexual. As a result, these couples frequently avoid small demonstrations of affection because of the fear that responding will lead to sex. Remember, it is continual nonsexual affection that nurtures marriage. The expression of physical affection through sexual intercourse can be considered an affectionate "bonus" to ongoing nonsexual affection and a great marriage.

CHAPTER 9
Negotiating Financial Waters

THE KEY: Being on the same page about the meaning of money and how money is used can make room for you to focus on other aspects of your relationship.

F irst things first: Money *is not* the number one cause of divorce. When marital researchers tested this popular belief, they simply did not find evidence that money was the reason for divorce. As we discussed earlier, the way a couple works through challenges and differences determines happiness within marriage. Money is, however, one of the more common issues through which deeper, unproductive problem-solving patterns can surface.

Five topics or issues dominate most couples' fights:

- sex
- money
- in-laws
- parenting
- leisure time

Like the other hot topics, money is just an avenue for the surfacing of relational issues. When couples come to therapy to resolve their "money problems," they start to notice challenges in other hot topic areas as they begin to discuss finances.

In this chapter, you will not find specific financial advice on investments, savings or checking accounts, or debt consolidation. Many books, as well as well-trained financial planners and consultants, can assist you with specific counsel concerning your own financial situation. Instead, we will discuss how to get to the bottom of your financial differences and to build from there. Many couples are surprised to learn that their money differences frequently have very little to do with money directly and a lot to do with their beliefs, values, and expectations.

The key to working through financial differences is to (1) resolve any conflict patterns that already exist, (2) understand what money means to you and your spouse, and (3) make financial plans considering both points of view.

Core Financial Filters

We all know that money is required to live. We all need food, clothing, transportation, and shelter. Money is our barter for these necessities, as well as for hobbies, retirement, vacations, savings, credit, and so on. Each person has beliefs, values, and expectations regarding the necessities listed above. Do not assume that your filters are the same as your spouse's. (See chapter 4 on "filters.")

Like all filters, your financial filters are like layers of an onion, building on each other. The more central the filter, the more it impacts every other filter built around it. The deeper levels of the onion tend to be beliefs and expectations that influence every aspect of life and your relationship.

A core filter may be an expectation that you need security, or, conversely, that you need to "live in the moment." Consider the priority list below:

Saving a little
Spontaneity
We have time
Live in the moment

No priorities have been applied to this list, so it is a jumbled mess. As an example let's say that one spouse desires fun and the other desires security. Let's see what happens to each spouse's priority list once we apply the filters.

Fun
Saving a little
Spontaneity
We have time
Live in the moment

Security
Saving
Planning
Retirement
Sacrifice

Now each priority list seems appropriate and perfectly understandable given the core filters of each person. To the spouse desiring security, saving only a little is going to seem financially irresponsible and shortsighted. To the spouse whose priority is having fun, saving a large part of the budget for a rainy day seems stupid; after all, what good is money in savings when you could be using it now to spend time together on hobbies, dates, and movies?

To ask spouses to try to understand their partner's perceptions seems unrealistic, since the filters driving each person's perceptions are so strong. Instead, both partners must compromise and sacrifice for a resolution. One spouse might not get to save as much as they would like, and the other may have to live with some boredom and lack of spontaneity.

Financial Expectations Activity

The word-association game below provides a way for you to make your financial expectations more explicit. We have provided some space for you to write your answers, but keep some spare paper handy in case you need more room. For each of the terms that we will list after the example, please jot down the following:

1. Your first thoughts (one sentence only)
2. Your feelings (a couple of words)
3. A specific example or scenario that illustrates your view

Here are the answers that one couple gave when asked to complete this task with the word *budget*.

The word is: *Budget*

Thoughts	Feelings	Specific Actions
Wise idea	Liberated	Sit down at the beginning of the month; see how much money we have coming in. Compare that to our incoming bills. Save 50% of the excess.

cont.

Thoughts	Feelings	Specific Actions
We're responsible, we don't need a budget.	Trapped, suffocated	Sit down at the beginning of the month; see how much money we have coming in. Compare that to our incoming bills. Save 25% of the excess.

Notice that the budget specifics for this couple are very similar. However, the word *budget* triggered deep emotional responses in each spouse; so deep, in fact, that they would start to argue before they even got to specifics. They actually ended up striking *budget* from their vocabulary because it was so emotionally laden for each of them. Instead, they talked about their "monthly plan."

Make your own worksheet with spaces to include your thoughts, feelings, and specific actions about the following words: Budget, Savings, Security, Retirement, Needs (necessities), Wants, Credit Card, Debt, Priorities, Surplus.

As you look through the Thoughts and Feelings columns, you may find a common thread that ties the terms together. This thread could explain your examples in the Specific Actions column. The common thread is a core filter. Let's peel away the layers of onion to identify your core filter. The outer layer of the onion is what you normally talk about with your spouse. The next layer down is what you have just done with this exercise, separating thoughts, feelings, and specifics.

Your Financial Orientation

When it comes to the next level of *financial filters*, three main categories have been identified by respected financial analyst Suze Orman. As you read about these three categories of filters, think about which category best describes your responses. (You may find that you have responses that fit into each category; that's fine, but prioritize them by determining which category has the most responses, then the second most, and finally the third most.)

(1) People—relationally oriented. The people in your life and the quality of those relationships are a high priority for you.

(2) Money—financially oriented. How money is saved, spent, and invested is a high priority for you.

(3) Things—object oriented. Having things now is a high priority for you. You believe the saying, "He with the most toys, wins."

If you have trouble determining which category your core filter falls in, answer the following questions:

• How do you spend your free time?
• What do you connect to your sense of "okayness," or identity/value, as a person?

The Relationally-Oriented Financial Filter

A relationally-oriented person typically says, "As long as we aren't massively in debt, I don't care about money; I just want to be with my family/spouse/friends." Spending usually centers on people-oriented activities such as dates, parties, and entertaining. For relationally-oriented individuals, financial security and material goods come after interpersonal relationships on the priority list. If the pursuit of money or stuff gets in the way of the relationships, "It just isn't worth it."

On the other hand, relationally-oriented people may spend enormous amounts of money if they believe that the expenditure will strengthen or enrich their relationships. If you purchased this book, relationships may be a high priority for you; after all, you're spending your free time reading a marital self-help book! Do you enjoy planning parties? Dates? Belonging to organizations because you like the people?

People that are relationally oriented tend to judge their sense of "okayness," or worth, by the quality of the relationships in their life. The better their relationships, the more comfortable they are with themselves.

Some core filters that drive this orientation are the needs for connection or intimacy, validation, and respect. Because of these core filters, arguments about money lead to a broad spectrum of outcomes, from "my way or the highway" on one end, to completely capitulating to the spouse's financial beliefs and expectations on the other end. Couples polarized at either end of the spectrum need help with their relationship. You may find that wherever your financial attitude falls on that continuum, it may repeat itself in other areas that challenge your marital relationship.

An excessive need for validation or respect tends to push individuals toward the "my way or the highway" end of the spectrum. An excessive need for connection tends to push people toward, the "I don't care what happens as long as I have you" end of the spectrum.

The middle of the spectrum enables open dialogue and respectful discussion. In this area, ideas and beliefs aren't as connected to the person's worth or identity. The most important question in discussions is, "What is best for our relationship?" Most of the time, the best thing for your relationship is a compromise, which may open up financial options that you have never considered before because your filter wouldn't allow it.

You may be tempted to use, "[My way] is best for the relationship" to get what you want. Please don't try that angle. Your spouse will likely feel invalidated, disregarded, and disconnected if you do this, and it will absolutely eat away at your relationship. Using your relationship as a weapon in financial discussions is unwise.

The Financially-Oriented Financial Filter

For financially-oriented people, money is a numbers game. They feel great joy in watching savings or investments grow, and an equal amount of pain when things turn sour. Their financial situation matters more than the amount of stuff they have. The wealthy person who drives a very modest vehicle, or the regular-guy neighbor worth millions of dollars, is probably financially oriented and definitely not object oriented.

So, how do you spend your free time? Do you read about investing tips, financial management, or business solutions? Do you spend more time at work than is required even though it isn't necessary to cover your financial obligations?

A person who gains a sense of okayness—positive self-worth—from this orientation tends to equate his or her financial worth to their overall worth as a person. The more money they accumulate, the more personal worth they have. People with this orientation run the risk of neglecting their personal relationships; they may even deny some of the nice things of life to themselves and others.

Some core filters that drive the financially-oriented person are the needs for influence, predictability, and security. People with these core filters must exercise caution. Left unchecked, these needs tend to lead to anxiety and controlling behaviors that can start to erode intimacy and closeness in marriage. As the relationship becomes less predictable and stable, the spouse tries to gain more control, which can decrease the quality of connection between spouses. And on it goes in a nasty cycle.

The Object-Oriented Financial Filter

Object-oriented people tend to tie their self-image to the material things they have. The more stuff they have, especially "in" stuff, the more adequate and positive they feel about themselves. There is nothing wrong with having some nice things. However, an object-oriented person may spend the majority of their free time thinking about or shopping for their next purchase.

They may not need anything and will still go shopping and make purchases. Are you going into debt for more stuff? Is shopping and purchasing more stuff getting in the way of your relationships? If you answered yes to either of those questions, you probably are object oriented.

The core filters that drive this orientation are the needs for self-worth and self-identity. The irony is that stuff, no matter how expensive, will never completely satisfy a need for self-worth. All it takes is an accident or natural disaster to take it all away. The satisfaction of having something nice lasts for a time, but then something new comes along. Object-oriented people tend toward a cycle of severe debt and an even greater sense of worthlessness.

You are of worth because you have a place on this earth. Most people derive a true sense of identity and worth from religious and spiritual beliefs that connect them to a higher power and from service to others that emanates from such beliefs.

Conclusion

The key to keeping your marital relationship healthy and functional in the financial aspects and avoiding significant debt is correctly prioritizing these three financial orientations or financial filters. We suggest that you place them in the following order:

1. Relationships
2. Finances
3. Objects

Any time object orientation comes before financial orientation, a couple has a recipe for debt. If finances or objects are more important than relationships, spouses risk marital failure.

It does seem simple to do. Once you and your spouse have identified your core filters and have compromised to balance them, together you will be able to have more constructive conversations and actually overcome financial challenges.

Below are four common-sense financial steps that you can take as a couple:

STEP #1 : DISCUSS YOUR fINANCIAL SITUATION REGULARLY, AT LEAST ON A WEEKLY BASIS.

Typically, one partner is "in charge" of the finances. If you are that person, invite your spouse to sit down with you as you pay bills and balance the checkbook. If you are not "in charge," ask to be involved. In one marriage, the wife is in charge of the finances. She calls her husband almost daily to balance the checkbook with her. He has Internet access to the checking account, so they both can find out where they are financially.

Step #2: Set financial goals together.

If you do not have any financial goals, you will constantly wonder, "Where did the money go?" Goals keep you focused and help you track your finances more diligently so you know where your money goes.

Step #3: Practice delayed gratification.

We live in a world of instant gratification, with feelings of, "I want it now." And it is easy to have it now, even if we do not need it. Recall a time when you shopped for furniture, an appliance, or a car, and the salesperson asked, "What payment can you afford?" After some negotiation, the monthly payment may have seemed so low that you made a major purchase on impulse. This is the kiss of death in financial management. Eventually you pay—with interest. Save money for what you want, or budget ahead for the purchase, and then make the purchase only when you have the amount needed. A new set of golf clubs is not an emergency and therefore can be saved for rather than immediately purchased. Try to classify each desired purchase into one of three categories: 1) Need for living, 2) Can improve living, 3) Luxury. The secret is being honest with yourself and spouse when trying to categorize your desired purchase. A vehicle may be a "Need for living." However, a reliable used car within your budget may suffice that need. A new car, when you already have one that works just fine, may fall in category two, "Can improve living." A new car with a high-end brand, or a new car with all the bells and whistles would fall into the "luxury" category.

Once categorized, you will be in a better position to determine when and how the purchase can or should be made.

Step #4: Balance freedom and connection.

Before you were married, you were "your own person," probably with complete control over your finances and unaccountable to anyone else. Now that you are married, your financial decisions affect your spouse, so you should plan jointly in financial matters. There isn't really a way around it, yet having a sense of financial freedom is important. Couples in great marriages have some money set aside, or budgeted, every week or month for each partner to spend on what he or she wants, no questions asked. This "guilt free" money gives each spouse a sense of freedom, recognizes individual choice, and enhances the connection and respect between husband and wife.

The financial arena is no different from any other challenge in marriage. Be mindful of how your financial filters, or priorities, are affecting your discussions of financial matters. Put what is best for the relationship first, financial goals and savings second, and stuff (things) last.

Chapter 10

Parenting Can Strengthen Your Marriage

THE KEY: No matter the age of the child, strong marriages can be made stronger when children are in the picture.

The moment you find out that you are expecting a child, whether by birth or adoption, a new interaction cycle starts to form between you as a couple. Interaction cycles look like a circle. There is no beginning; there is no end. Such an endless cycle exists between the child and your marriage. You will have the chance to create and form a person. That person will forever change your life. No longer are you only a couple; you are now a family.

Children can definitely distract you from your marriage. You won't be able to spend as much time as a couple as you did before. Spontaneity seems to all but vanish as you have several schedules and needs to account for. Even after the children are grown and out of the house, they are still involved in your life.

Bringing children into your family is a lot like starting a new exercise program. When you exercise, you know that it is a great thing, but are you ever sore for the next few days! You're sore because you were using muscles you could have sworn didn't exist. Yet, the muscle pain is a sign that you are getting stronger. This is similar to the affect children will have on the strength of your marriage. Children will push your relationship in places it couldn't go any other way. If you choose to hang in there and keep flexing those new marital muscles, you will adapt and be stronger for it.

One thing that many people don't realize is that the quality of your marriage is actually a big part of parenting. More and more research is finding that children's well-being, scholastic achievement, and problem-solving skills are connected to the psychological and emotional health of their parents' marriage. The more effectively you work through problems as a couple, the more your children will be able to work through problems. Kids learn enormous amounts by watching what you do. By keeping your marriage a priority, your children will benefit from this throughout their whole lives.

Managing the Transition to Parenthood

One of the most difficult transitions that happens to couples when they are expecting a baby, or after the child is born, is the shift of focus away from each other. This is a time where everyone is shifting in their roles and adding new ones. You are now more than a spouse; you are also a parent. Unfortunately, you don't get to add any extra time to your day to compensate for your extra roles. Below is some specific advice for each of you to aid you through this transition.

For Dad

It is common for husbands to feel left out and in some cases neglected as their wives become more focused on the baby. The thing you need to remember is that her behavior does not mean she doesn't need you or love you. In fact, it may mean the opposite. She may feel secure enough in your relationship that she trusts that you love her. That frees her up to focus on the child.

One of the best things you can do to connect with your wife during this time is to learn about how the baby is developing, both prenatally and after birth. Ask your sweetheart questions about how she is feeling physically and emotionally. It is common for women to feel apprehensive about becoming a mother. If that is the case, some kind reassurance will go a long way to build her up.

She doesn't want to do this on her own. Focusing on her and the baby's needs during this time will pay innumerable dividends in the long run. Think of it as a long-term investment in your marriage. It will pay off. The best part is that you will be able to experience an amazing side to your wife that you would not be able to see any other way.

For Mom

Your natural instincts will cause you to put much of your focus on the baby, as they should. One thing to remember is that your husband doesn't feel any of the physical and emotional changes that you are going through. All he knows is that you are pregnant or just had the baby. He will not know anything unless you tell him. Share how you feel with him. Don't be afraid to ask for help. Don't be afraid to ask questions about his experience. You don't have to do this all on your own. The more you can include your husband, the more he will attach to the baby.

One of the best things you can do is to express appreciation for his support. Giving him feedback on what you appreciate will go a long way to let him know that you need him. He will then be more likely to repeat those actions that you have told him you appreciate.

Staying Married with Children

One of the best things to remember in marriage is the "big picture." That is especially true when children come into the family. The big picture tells you that the children will grow up and become adults with families of their own. As children grow up and leave home, you will have more time to be with each other. If you haven't found a way to enrich your marriage all along the way, what will you have when it is just the two of you again?

It is appropriate that much of your energy and focus is on the children and their needs, especially when they are young. That being said, try to spend at least 15 to 20 minutes a day talking just with your sweetheart. This will be important in sustaining your marital relationship until the time when it is only the two of you in the house again.

Try to spend the time talking about your thoughts, feelings, and reactions to the various things that have happened during the day that may or may not be related to the children. If one of you is a full-time parent, talking about something besides the children may be difficult. Discussing your thoughts, feelings, and hopes in regards to the children will be more powerful than just a news report of the day's agenda. The more you talk with each other, the more you will connect, and the more you can enjoy each other and your children. Talking about current events on the national, state, and local stage is one way to have "adult" conversation that stay-at-home parents sometimes so desperately desire.

Find Time to Keep Courting

We recommend a weekly date night throughout the years of your marriage. For fun, we included seven signs that "you need to go on a date."

- When you hear someone else's baby cry, you start rocking back and forth.
- You know what a Chernobyl diaper is.
- You have an in depth discussion for 20 minutes with your partner about the Chernobyl diaper.
- When you hug each other, you try to burp your sweetheart.
- You have soccer practice, piano lessons, a dance recital, and a PTA meeting all at the same time. (That was just your Monday schedule!)
- The last "gourmet" dinner you can remember consisted of mac and cheese.
- Spontaneity, what's that? How can I work that into my schedule?

As you court during your marriage, try not to assume you already "know" your partner. Be curious. Ask open-ended questions. What would you want to know about your sweetheart if you'd never met before? Where does your spouse see himself in five, ten, or fifteen years? This way you will be open to wonderful surprises and changes in your partner. You will also be less likely to be staring at a stranger across the table when the children are gone.

Where Is the Source of Your Parenting?

No matter how old the children are, there are some basic sources from which people parent. Parents will tend to either base the way they respond to their children's needs out of *love* or *fear*. In an ideal setting, fear and love do not coexist. In reality, we parent out of some combination of the two. Hopefully, people are moving to parent out of love more and more. Effective parents will have concerns about their children and how their children will face particular challenges, such as when their child is offered drugs or alcohol, when they apply for their first loan, or whom they decide to marry. Having concerns and helping children to face the challenges of life is essential in parenting. The difference between parenting out of love and parenting out of fear comes in how you approach your children with those concerns. Your approach will be rooted in fear or love.

Parenting Out of Fear

Parenting from fear will tend to lead parents to extremes. One extreme is when parents are overly controlling and punishing. They are going to "make" their children become perfect adults! They don't want their children to go through the same problems as they or some of their friends went through. When these parents think about the possibility of their children going through painful situations, they go into a panic. The mere thought of their children hurting in the future is unbelievably painful for them.

These parents are consistently responding to the "what ifs," the "what might happens," and "what will people think?" They are parenting so that their children will be insulated from life's pain. They are also parenting so they themselves won't experience the pain or embarrassment of watching their children make mistakes. Parenting out of fear ends up being as much, or more, about the parents' needs as the child's.

The irony of parenting out of fear is that such parents will often create the very situations they were hoping to avoid. Many of you will simply need to remember your adolescence to illustrate this point. Then again, you probably were the "angel" child, right? It never ceases to amaze us that when asked as adults, over 90 percent of you would say that you were the "perfect teen." If we were to ask your parents, 90 percent of them would have called you anything but "perfect."

A couple we'll call Peggy and Dean both grew up in homes where one parent struggled with alcoholism. They were determined that their children would stay away from the same trap. When their children were little, they taught them the "evils" of alcohol. Peggy and Dean told their children how alcohol had "destroyed" their grandparents. At every turn, they rehearsed "just say no" with them. Every "evil" and "vice" of the world could be traced to alcohol.

Their oldest son, Scott, grew up in this environment. When he came home from any extracurricular event, he was grilled by his parents on whether or not he had been drinking. All Scott ever heard was about the "evils" of alcohol. When he was hanging out with his other thirteen-year-old friends one day, one of them had a beer for everyone to try. They told Scott that it may taste bad at first but it was really "relaxing" and "cool." Scott thought, "It can't be as bad as Mom and Dad said."

When his parents found out he had tried a beer, they grounded Scott for a month and banned him from those friends. Surely that would "teach" him that they were serious about the evils of alcohol. A few years later, Scott was in recovery from alcoholism himself, and his parents were confused. They had taught him the "right" way, hadn't they? While their intentions were good, they had parented in a way that they were trying to control their fear as much as they were trying to parent Scott. Severe grounding felt like a relief for them as parents.

All Scott learned was to hide his drinking to avoid punishment.

The other side of parenting out of fear is inaction. Parents with this problem are paralyzed by potential conflict with their children. These kids get to run everywhere they want. There are few rules in the house. "They're just being kids," the parents say. Fear in this setting comes out in an attitude that says, "as long as the kids are happy" because delivering consequences "aren't worth the fight." Rules out of this kind of parenting are frequently based on the situation and mood of the parent. Sometimes the parent will be very strict if little Johnny hits Sally. Other times Johnny hits Sally and everyone laughs. Kids in these families learn that if they have tantrums long enough, and loud enough, they will get what they want. They become masters of bribing their parents with good behavior to get what they want. These parents many times report that "Life will be a tough enough teacher; I need to be there for my child as their friend."

After their struggles with Scott, Peggy and Dean decided to take a different approach with their youngest daughter, Sandy. They thought if they could be Sandy's friend, they would be in more of a position to help her stay away from alcohol. Everything was negotiated with Sandy from the time she was little. Consequences were negotiated or nonexistent. Rewards were negotiated. As long as Sandy was happy, that was all that mattered.

Then Sandy hit adolescence. She was allowed to set her own curfew and hang out with any crowd she wanted. When her parents started to try to give her consequences for her behavior, it became World War Three. They backed down to her threats of leaving home (some fear-based parenting here) because they thought it wasn't worth the fight. They felt it was better to at least have her at home so they would know what she was doing. A few years of that and Sandy was entering rehab while Dean and Peggy entered marriage counseling.

Parenting Out of Love

Parenting out of love is 100 percent child-focused. The needs of the children are paramount. Children's wants are considered in terms of the "big picture." In other words, wants are considered in terms of the overall parenting goals. Parenting out of love requires the parents to understand the capabilities and interests of each child and their current stage of development. Consequences are given in consistent and appropriate ways.

People who parent out of love allow their children to be children. Kids will embarrass you in public. They will make mistakes. They will get hurt and may hurt others. They are a source of many of your greatest joys as well as many of your greatest disappointments. It's all in their job description. The best thing you can do to parent out of love is to separate to some extent how you rate your effectiveness as a parent from your child's successes and failures. Easier said than done, we know.

The reason it is important to have some separate criteria for judging your effectiveness as a parent is that it starts to eliminate fear. If you want feedback on how you are parenting, your sweetheart can be a great source for you. Just be careful what you ask for! At some point, a child's mistake needs to be reflective of their behavior—not of your failings or successes as a parent. You've heard that you're not supposed to blame your parents for your problems, right? So then why would you blame yourself for all of your children's choices?

So then, what are you responsible for as parents? You are responsible for the environment the children grow up in. It is much like a gardener is responsible for providing nourishing soil, water, and a patch of ground accessible to the sun. The gardener will also remove any weeds while the seedling is young. A gardener will also adapt the environment based on what kind of seed has been planted. As the plant gets bigger, many of the weeds will not be a threat to it anymore. As the child grows, she becomes more independent and is able to make bigger decisions consulting with her parents rather than her parents deciding for her. The environment for each child may need to be adapted to meet his or her needs.

To start parenting out of love, discuss the following questions with your spouse:

- What are your children's dreams?
- What are their interests, talents, hobbies?
- Describe "appropriate discipline" using specific examples.
- What kind of relationship skills do you want your children to have?
- What kind of consequences have been the most effective for each child?
- Which consequences were out of the best interest of the child?
- Which consequences were out of your fear?
- What are your thoughts about extracurricular activities?
- What are your thoughts about dating?
- Who are your child's friends?
- What do you think about your child's friends?
- What do you want for your child academically?
- What kind of spirituality or religion do you want to be part of your child's life?
- What are some of your fears as a parent?

The last question was included because as you are able to identify your fears, you will be in a better position to do something different. When you find yourself parenting out of fear, stop. Remember that when you parent out of fear, the tendency is going to be to try to force, control, or not engage at all. We are not saying that your child isn't doing something inappropriate. It is how you address the inappropriate behavior that makes the difference. Parenting out of love will tend to teach, or help the child find answers for himself. Giving consequences can teach as well.

When approaching a "teaching moment," ask yourself the following questions. These questions are appropriate to ask yourself even if the child is an adult:

- What does the child need right now (validation, listening, correction)?
- What kind of understanding does the child have that what they have done that is inappropriate?
- What kind of approach does the child respond to the best?
- Is this a moment to for me to talk or listen? (Tip: Try listening first, especially with teens.)
- Is this a new situation for the child or one he's encountered before?
- What consequence, if any are needed, is appropriate for the situation?
- Are there natural consequences that you can use?
- Does the child know the consequences for *appropriate* behavior in the same situation?

It will be easier to answer these questions when you are not "in the moment." Taking some time to answer these questions about past parenting experiences will provide valuable practice.

Comment on Infertility

Many couples are unable to have biological children of their own for a variety of reasons. There are many of you who would love nothing more than to have a child, yet cannot become pregnant. Infertility can be a particularly difficult challenge for couples to face. It can be an opportunity for you to pull together as a couple—for you to work together for a common goal and purpose.

It is natural to feel discouraged, powerless, hopeless, and full of grief. Obviously, stay away from blaming the spouse who may have a medical problem leading to infertility. Physicians tell us that 50 percent of fertility problems are male and 50 percent are female. Self-blame also becomes a temptation in this situation. Either way, blame can be toxic to any marriage.

If it turns out that you are not able to have a biological child of your own, it is appropriate to grieve that loss. As you grieve and experience this unexpected event, other options may become open to you that you hadn't thought of before. It is crucial to maintain hope and confront the frustration of infertility as much as possible. Hope and optimism will help each of you feel psychologically and physically healthier and is a means to enrich your marriage.

Wrapping It Up

Being parents can bring a depth to your marriage that is impossible to achieve any other way. You will affect your children—no matter their age—for immeasurable good. Taking time for your marriage will keep you connected to each other and give your children (even adult children) a sense of security and a model of marriage to follow. When you approach any relationship from a source of love, you will be a positive force in their lives. Happy parenting!

CHAPTER 11
Dealing with Crises

THE KEY: Husbands and wives in successful marriages are able to manage the inevitable crises that occur in life and use those experiences to strengthen their marriage.

L ife happens. That's true whether it is an earthquake, hurricane, car accident, or cancer. Sooner or later, you will be caught off guard by some event and will probably question "What now?" or "Why me?" Crises can come in many forms. Some are expected; some are not. Either way, those events and experiences will profoundly affect you and your marriage—for better or worse.

Crises can have a unifying power to those who were involved. When you share an intense emotional experience with another person, that experience can bind you together for a lifetime. Almost any crisis can strengthen the ties between you to your sweetheart if you allow it to. Since crises will come, luckily there are some things you can do individually and as a couple that will utilize these crises to your benefit!

What Is a "Crisis"?

The short answer is "any event or experience that you perceive to be a crisis." The key word in this sentence is *perceive*. If someone perceives an event to be a crisis, then that is what it is for that person. A more specific answer of what constitutes a crisis is "an event or experience that you don't think you have the knowledge, skills, or resources to handle." Again, the phrase "you don't think" refers to how you perceive yourself and the situation.

This definition of what constitutes a crisis is the reason why a married couple can go through a destructive house fire due to a short circuit in an appliance, and one person handles it as if it were a minor inconvenience while the other person is incapacitated for weeks afterward. Each person perceives the experience differently. For one, the experience may have been a setback, yet also an opportunity to start over. For the other person, their life is over. They think that they will never recover from it. Guess what? They are both right. They will both likely find what they are looking for. This kind of crisis would be a result of an unfortunate accident, possibly because of someone else's choices (for example, not replacing a faulty appliance). Below are listed the different kind of crises that can happen on a regular basis, and what you can do about them.

Type 1: Crises as a Result of Our Own Choices

In many ways, these crises can be the most painful. The crisis is a direct consequence of a choice, or a series of choices, that can all be traced back to one person—you. Some examples of these kinds of crises include:

- Bankruptcy due to living beyond your means.
- Loss of job because you were intentionally negligent in your duties or lost your temper.

- Illness or disease because you did not follow medical advice or wisdom.
- Divorce or pain because you chose to give your marriage low priority.

Crises that are a result of our own choices also have a lot of hope attached to them, however. There is hope because you can change the behavior that put you into the crisis in the first place. After all, it was you who got yourself into the situation; it is you who will get you out of the situation.

Not every crisis is the result of poor decisions, however. There are numerous cases where people put themselves in a position to be very successful, yet at some point in the process of moving forward, they realize there is a chance to fall—or worse yet, fail. In these situations, people become like tightrope walkers who all of the sudden look down at the ground instead of what they are supposed to be focusing on.

Type 2: Crises as a Result of Another's Choices
Some crises occur because someone else makes a decision that directly affects you and causes a crisis. Some examples of these crises include:

- Theft or robbery
- Layoffs at work
- Child abuse
- Domestic violence
- Rape
- Drunk driving accident
- Terrorist attack such as September 11th

When these kinds of events occur, most people are left confused and often ask themselves, "Why did they do that to me?" These events often happen without notice and without you exercising any choice in the matter.

Feelings of powerlessness are a normal reaction in these situations. So are thoughts of, "It's not fair!" These kinds of events are *not* fair, yet they happen. Acknowledging that what happened was wrong or hurt you is important. Grieving goes a long ways in helping navigate these crises as well. Grieving "what should be," or "what should have been" will enable you to shift gears and start picking up the pieces. Focusing on the past event will continue to leave you in a position of powerlessness. Grieving will help shift the focus from the past and into the present and future.

Type 3: "Acts of God" or Mother Nature

These events are similar to crises initiated by the choice of someone else, in that you have no control over whether they happen or not. Mother Nature can pack an unimaginable punch in destroying life and material possessions. Other kinds of crises that fit in this section are health related. Here is a brief list of crises that fit in this category:

- Earthquakes
- Hurricanes
- Tornadoes
- Flash floods
- Cancer
- Diabetes
- Leukemia
- Infertility

The feelings of insignificance and powerlessness in the face of

Mother Nature's fury are to be expected. You can prepare the best you can for such disasters and then the rest of it is up nature. There is no rhyme or reason why in natural disasters some homes are destroyed and others are not. As discussed previously, coming to some level of acceptance of the event through grieving will help make the transition into picking up the pieces and moving on with life.

When it comes to medical crises, the initial diagnosis is one of the most difficult times. No one wants to hear that they have a lifelong disease or life-threatening illness. The initial shock and the feeling of "What do I do now?" is common for everyone. Again, grieving initially is appropriate and incredibly helpful in managing the emotions of the situation. Once you can grieve the loss and "what should have been" or "what you wish would have been," the shift of focus to "what can my life be like now" will lead to a life rich in possibility.

For those who have insurance in some form, it will be a huge relief for all of these kinds of events. Insurance provides some sense of security—it can replace homes or help pay for expensive medical treatments. Preparation in the form of 72-hour kits can also take the edge off many of these events. A 72-hour kit is a bag or pack with food, water, personal items, medical supplies, and clothing for everyone in the house that will get you through three days. Keeping an active and healthy lifestyle will also help you face any crises with more confidence and you will be in a better condition to deal with it. The key to preparation is to prepare the best you can and then live your life! Living in constant fear may actually induce some medical problems. Living in constant fear will also get in the way of seeing the wonders and beauty of life.

Type 4: Life Transitions

We all went through different stages of development as we were growing up. You went through a stage as an infant, toddler, preschooler, grade-schooler, adolescent, and then finally became an adult. Marriage and family life has a developmental cycle as well. The stages of this cycle are marked by different events. Each event can be a crisis for some individuals and families. Below is a list of such events:

- When you left home to be on your own
- Marriage
- Arrival of first child
- Children becoming adolescents
- "Launching" your children out of the house
- Empty nest
- Divorce
- Death of parents, other family members, friends
- Death of your sweetheart

Each stage of family life is characterized by a transition. Each transition can be viewed as an opportunity. If you stay stuck wishing you were back in the previous stages (or wishing you were in the future stages), you will miss the moments of happiness that are occurring now. Most people are naturally apprehensive about change. As you move into each stage, there is a period of confusion and adjustment that takes place. It is the same when you are learning a new dance—everyone is stepping on toes and it is awkward. The secret to learning a new dance is to go slower, be very intentional in your movements, and talk to each other a lot. Then you eventually speed up until it is "easy." You can do the same when moving through the potential crises of family transitions. Be very intentional in how you respond and talk about the issue a lot. It might be awkward at first, but then everyone will start to adjust to the new "dance" and it will become second nature.

Anticipated versus Unanticipated

Any of the four types of crises will happen in one of two ways. Either you will be expecting them and they are *anticipated*, or they will catch you off guard and they will be *unanticipated*. Each type has its advantages and disadvantages, depending on the person.

ANTICIPATED

An anticipated crisis can be prepared for. You can make plans and organize resources to compensate for the changes that will occur. Many of the transitions in family development are anticipated. Getting some education and communicating with all involved prior to the crisis will go a long way in easing these transitions.

We know that many natural disasters are now being predicted more accurately than just a few years ago. That being said, most people will not have time to prepare for the disaster once the warning has been given. Having an escape plan and supplies on hand before the crisis occurs will make it easier when the warning does come. Get to know what disasters your area is most prone to and plan accordingly

The downside of knowing a crisis (medical or environmental) is coming is that it becomes easy to start living in fear of the event. This is especially problematic when you don't know when or if the event will happen. Reminding yourself that you have done what you can helps ease any anxiety that you might experience about an uncertain event.

UNANTICIPATED

Unanticipated or unexpected crises are difficult because you have no warning they are coming. Transportation accidents are a good example of unexpected crises. The unexpected terrorist attacks of September 11th also come to mind as an unexpected crisis that affected our country. Shock is typically the first response to unexpected events. Then the realization of what happened starts to sink in and sadness, hurt, and anger frequently follow. As those emotions start to become less pronounced, you are then in a position to start working through the aftermath of the unexpected crisis.

Steps to Manage a Crisis

What follows are general steps for you to use when trying to navigate any crisis. We have also included a worksheet at the end of this chapter that you can use to work through these steps. As each step is discussed, you will find a corresponding section on the worksheet for you to write your thoughts. It would be a great exercise for you and your partner to do together, even if you just talk about each section of the worksheet rather than filling it in.

BREATHE!

Having a strong emotional reaction is normal during and after a difficult situation. However, be careful not to make major decisions when you are in that state of mind. Your mind and perception will be clouded by the crisis. Do the best you can to calm down and clear your head. First, talk with your spouse and then perhaps talk to a trusted friend, family member, ecclesiastical leader, or professional therapist who can help give you some perspective on decisions of how to move forward.

Crises have a way of skewing your perception of what life is like or what has happened. It is tempting to assume that your life will always be like it is during the crisis. That is not true at all. The trial that a crisis brings is only a moment in your life, not your life itself. Take some time and make a list of what you do have going for you. These things will be easy to discount or not to take seriously if you are in the middle of a crisis. That is one way the crisis can warp your perception. Force yourself to look at what you have going for you. Most of those things on the list are currently present and will be present in the future.

Determine What Kind of Crisis You Are Facing

Look through or think of the four types of crises. Is the current situation something that is a result of your own choice? Is it a result of someone else's choice? Is it an act of God? Or is it a life transition? Now determine whether this crisis came out of the blue or was anticipated.

By determining what kind of event you are experiencing, you will be in a better position to work through it. As the old philosophy goes, "If you can name it, you can change it." You can't erase the crisis, but you *can* work to have the life that is possible from this point on.

Identify Your Resources

A "resource" is anything or anyone that will be able to help you manage the event you are experiencing. Make a list of what resources you may have. Here is a list of resources you could consider:

- Experiential—Have you, or has someone close to you, had a similar experience? What can you take from that experience that will help you through this one?
- Emotional—Your emotions can be a resource to you. If expressed appropriately, your emotions will allow you to let go of

negative tension as well as to connect to those around you. Read chapter 16, "Managing Your Emotions," to find more information on how you can manage your emotions more effectively.

- Cognitive—Your ability to think is absolutely a resource. This becomes an even greater asset as you manage your emotions more effectively. The process of problem solving is an intellectual exercise for the most part; allow your cognitive skills to be a huge resource.

- Material—Your financial assets can be a resource to you. This would include any insurance policies you have. It would also include your vehicle, home, computer, and so on.

- Skills and Knowledge Base—Anything you have inside of you in terms of your knowledge and skills fits in this category. For example, you may be a superb computer technician, accountant, or caregiver. Your skills and knowledge base goes wherever you go.

- Other People—This is one of your most powerful resources in managing a crisis. Identify at least three people (the more the better) who will be able to help you through the crisis. Your spouse should be first on your list! Make a list of how they can be helpful. The next step is the tough part. Swallow your pride and ask for the help!

Match Your Resources with Your Needs

Now that you have made a list of your resources, how do they match up with the needs of the situation? Fitting resources to your current needs is the next step. Be creative! The matches may not be apparent at first, but they are there. Often this step is when new possibilities open up to you that you would never have seen before the crisis happened. This is the blessing of crises. Through the hardship you will find new, wonderful aspects of your life that will enrich your marriage and family.

Look at What Is Possible from This Point On

Now is the time to plan on where you can go from here. Look at what is possible now and in the future. The ironic thing is that you may overestimate what is possible in five years, but you will substantially underestimate what is possible in the next twenty. Ask yourself how this situation can benefit you or your marriage. As mentioned at the beginning of this chapter, any crises can bind people together and make relationships stronger. This step is your chance to identify specific ways in which the current situation can benefit you, your marriage, and your family. For example, in managing the transition of your oldest child into adolescence, you will learn some basic parenting techniques and approaches that can be used with your next child.

Get to It!

Now it is time to put everything together and go into action mode. If you follow these steps, you can more easily move through crises and come out stronger on the other side.

Wrapping It Up

Crises are rarely enjoyable when you are in the midst of them. Hopefully, in retrospect, those moments of your life will be part of the building blocks of your marriage. Navigating these difficult events together will bind you to each other if you let them. You will see sides of yourself and your sweetheart that you would not see any other way.

Prepare the best you can for possible events, and then focus back on your life. Remember, your life itself is not a crisis and it never will be a crisis. Crises are a *part* of life events, nothing more. By rallying your resources and relying on each other, you will make it.

Briefly describe the situation: _____

_____

_____

_____

_____.

Where does this situation fit in with the overall picture of your life?

_____

_____

_____

_____.

Put a check mark in the box or boxes that apply to the current situation.

☐ Your Choices   ☐ Life Transitions

☐ Another's Choices   ☐ Anticipated

☐ Acts of God   ☐ Unanticipated

What part(s) of the situation do you have any influence over?

_____

_____

_____

_____.

List your resources:_____
_____
_____
_____
_____.

List at least three people who could help you, and how they could help you through this situation.

1._____
2._____
3._____

How do your resources match up with the needs of the situation? Be creative!_____
_____
_____
_____
_____.

What can be possible from this point on?_____
_____
_____
_____
_____.

How can this situation benefit you and/or your marriage?_____
_____
_____
_____.

CHAPTER 12
A Look At Your Personalities

THE KEY: As a couple, understanding similarities and differences in your personality traits and interests helps keep your marriage strong.

Often we describe people in terms of their personal temperament—outgoing, quiet, happy, sad, productive, lazy, leader, follower, and so on. We might also describe a person according to their physical characteristics—short, tall, fat, skinny, and so on. Or their financial situation or achievements—rich, poor, and so on.

Today, assessing or measuring compatibility among people is trendy. This is particularly true with online computer dating services. Many commercials entice individuals to take a test or visit a website that matches people based on a compatibility instrument or questionnaire. The goal in doing so is generally to help two people discover whether they will be compatible marriage partners and whether their marriage will last.

This chapter will help you think about your and your spouse's personalities and temperament so you can understand how you are different from and similar to each other. It will not predict the outcome of your marriage; rather, it will give you an increased understanding of each other and an appreciation for each other in your marriage relationship.

Background Concepts

We will not delve into details regarding personality development and its influence on marriage. However some ideas do need a brief explanation.

1. Your choice of a mate is an expression of your personality.

Personality includes all sorts of traits and such things as needs, temperaments, and attitudes. Therefore, your personality is the major criterion or lens against which you select a mate. One of the intriguing and somewhat mystical aspects of mate selection is that it is a process of interactive and reciprocal selection. That is, selecting a marriage partner in Western society is not "going shopping," in which one person, the shopper, selects an object to purchase. The purchase responds totally to the shopper. Your mate selection process involved *two* shoppers, at least when it got to the purchase stage! During the process of mate selection, both partners are consciously and unconsciously "testing the waters." Mate selection is not an accidental or casual process. Rather, marriage results from powerful forces that impel the couple toward it. Couples approach marriage intentionally. Partners intentionally seek a spouse whom they like and believe that they can live with.

2. You can get an idea of your personality by thinking about the things that you enjoy doing, or given time, would enjoy doing.

In many ways, your personality is a reflection of your life experience and history. Consider your preferences, recreational activities, hobbies, and work that you enjoy. We tend to seek out and participate in activities that are enjoyable and meaningful to us.

3. *Happy couples tend to have complementary or balancing personalities.*

In some marriages spouses are similar, like "two peas in a pod." In other marriages, the spouses are very different. A simple matching or blending of personalities and temperaments does not, in itself, ensure a happy marriage. Instead, the way that the spouses interact and communicate their similarities and differences is the key to marital stability and satisfaction.

4. *Marital satisfaction, stability, and achievement also depend on the environment that couples create in their home and marriage.*

Married couples create their living environment. They create their home by fixing it up or designing and furnishing it so that it meets their needs and wishes. The sayings, "One's home is his castle," and "Home is a bit of heaven on earth" convey the importance of a couple's home in their life together. What does the home of a particular married couple look like? Where is their home? Does the couple prefer a rural or an urban environment? Does the couple prefer modern or traditional styles in architecture and furnishings? Answers to such questions as these can be one indication of the couple's personalities. In instances where couples either don't have much choice about their home's location/style, or don't agree on such issues, the key is what their dreams? How to handle differences in preference are not what we are discussing here and can be worked out another time.

A View of Six Personality Types—The Hexagon

Personality can be viewed many ways. Personality is a global concept that includes all sorts of traits, needs, temperaments, and attitudes. Personality is described with many labels. Some people describe personalities in psychological language (introverted, extroverted). Others depict personalities using colors (red = power, yellow = fun lover, blue = do-gooders, white = peace keepers). Still others use animals to characterize different personalities (lion = leader, otter = fun loving, golden retriever = server, beaver = worker).

One useful personality model identifies six categories or primary traits. This model can be illustrated with a hexagon. It was developed over forty years ago by Dr. John Holland and is theoretically and empirically based.

The hexagonal figure below shows the relationship of personality types to one another. Types that are closest together in the hexagon are more similar; types that are placed farther apart or across from each other are less similar or even opposites.

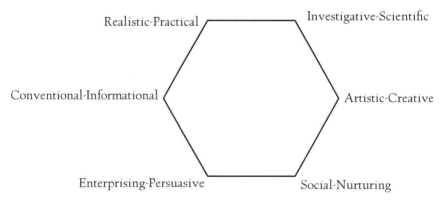

The six personality types are Realistic-Practical, Investigative-Scientific, Artistic-Creative, Social-Nurturing, Enterprising-Persuasive, and Conventional-Informational. As you can see in the figure, the types that are least similar to each other are further apart on the hexagon. For example, the Realistic-Practical and Social-Nurturing types, being diagonally opposite each other, are less alike than the Realistic-Practical and Conventional-Informational types, which, being adjacent to each other, are more similar.

We are using this model to illustrate how you and your spouse's likes and dislikes, preferences and aversions, make up your personalities. People prefer to spend their time in certain ways, whether at work or at leisure. They seek work and leisure activities that they enjoy and find fulfilling. Similarly, they tend to enjoy being around people with similar and complementary interests. Recall that during your early acquaintance and courtship with your spouse, you became aware of each other's similarities and differences in personality and preference for activities. Undoubtedly, some of these similarities in interests and activities helped move your relationship toward marriage.

Ask yourself the following questions, and then think about your responses:

- What do you enjoy doing?
- What aspects of your employment or work do you find enjoyable and fulfilling?
- What do you dislike about your work?
- What do you like to do, or would you like to do, in your leisure time?
- What sorts of activities do you like and dislike?
- What are you good at?
- Do you like to interact with people or not to be so involved with people?

• Do you prefer to be on the go or stay at home?

How would your spouse answer these questions? How do you see each other in relation to these questions? For example, what would you say your spouse likes to do in their leisure time? What are their competencies? Answering questions such as these will help you get in the frame of mind to think about the following personality types.

The brief descriptions of personality types that follow are intended to give you a sense of each of the six types. People's personalities have aspects of more than one type. As you look at each type, ask yourself, "To what extent am I, or my spouse, like this description? What does this type of person enjoy? What does this type of person prefer to do? What might this type of person be particularly good at? How might others describe this person?"

Realistic-Practical

The Realistic-Practical person enjoys activities that involve working with objects, machines, and tools. They like settings that require hands-on experience. A Realistic person would prefer to use practical approaches to solve problems rather than using social or interpersonal skills. Such a person might be particularly adept at building, maintaining, and repairing things, using tools such as a hammer and nails or a sewing machine. Realistic-Practical people are coordinated and often athletic. Others might describe a Realistic person as practical, sensible, wise, skillful, and somewhat shy. Typically, Realistic-Practical people are least like Social-Nurturing types and tend to avoid close interpersonal relationships. They see themselves as practical, persistent, somewhat unsociable, often submissive toward others' ideas, and perhaps having a somewhat narrow range of interests. They tend to avoid supervisory and leadership roles. A Realistic-Practical husband would be the ultimate handyman and fixer-upper.

Research shows that Realistic people gravitate to such occupations as electrician, carpenter, photographer, forest ranger, landscape gardener, laboratory technician, floral designer, mechanic, ambulance driver, sound technician, machinist, and cook. Leisure activities that Realistic people enjoy include gardening, knitting, wood turning, barbecuing, home repair, restoration of antiques, crocheting, doll making, camping, and other outdoor activities.

Investigative-Scientific

The Investigative-Scientific person enjoys activities that involve investigating and seeking to understand scientific and everyday functioning of people or things. Investigative people use inquiry, reason, and intuition to solve problems and understand events. They are very good at problem solving, particularly in situations that require intellectual and mathematical ability. However, the Investigative-Scientific type is not limited to laboratory scientists or crime scene investigators.

Others might describe the Investigative-Scientific person as curious, analytical, intellectual, introspective, methodical, critical, socially reserved, and somewhat shy. Investigative-Scientific people achieve principally in academic and scientific areas, where they can apply their creativity and intelligence. They see themselves as somewhat unsociable, independent, scholarly, introverted, able to generate original ideas, and somewhat aloof in interpersonal relationships. Typically, Investigative-Scientific people are least like Enterprising-Persuasive types.

Investigative-Scientific occupations often include physician, botanist, museum curator, exercise physiologist, meteorologist, chemist, airplane pilot, dentist, linguist, nurse anesthetist, astronomer, mathematician, and pharmacist. Enjoyable leisure activities include amateur radio, astrology, genealogy, board games, recreational flying, taxidermy, and the study of history.

Artistic-Creative

Artistic-Creative people enjoy activities that involve creating and expressing verbal, written, musical, performing, and visual art forms. They use language, art, music, drama, or writing to create and communicate concepts and ideas and to produce tangible objects. They tend to have exceptional perceptual and motor skills conducive to achievement and excellence in the arts.

Others describe the Artistic-Creative person as subjective, imaginative, impulsive, nonconforming, emotional, idealistic, and independent in judgment and thought. Artistic people describe themselves as sensitive, independent, flexible, either somewhat irresponsible or very responsible, neat, orderly, self-confident, and expressive. Typically, Artistic-Creative types are least like Conventional-Informational people.

Artistic-Creative people enjoy such occupations as model maker, stage technician, architect, artist, actor, book or newspaper editor, composer, poet, sculptor, orchestra member or conductor, illustrator, photographer, musician, art dealer, and wedding consultant. They like to spend their leisure time doing such things as decorating cakes, doing crossword puzzles, throwing ceramics, participating in cultural organizations, going to movies or the theater, singing, drawing, performing magic tricks, painting with oil and watercolors, and reading fiction.

Social-Nurturing

The Social-Nurturing person prefers activities that involve other people in positive and affirmative human relationships and interactions. This person uses social and interpersonal competencies and abilities to communicate with others. Social-Nurturing people have very good social skills, and they desire social interaction. In problem solving, Social people rely primarily on emotions and feelings. They tend to seek to understand other people rather than to focus on others understanding them.

Friends, family, or co-workers describe the Social-Nurturing person as helpful, kind, respectful, tactful, friendly, understanding, and idealistic. The Social person is very sensitive to the needs of others and wants to nurture them. In many ways, the Social personality amplifies characteristics of good parenting. Typically, Social-Nurturing people are least like Realistic-Practical people.

Social-Nurturing people enjoy occupations that require helping others, such as homemaker, dietitian, mail carrier, nurse, midwife, physical therapist, speech pathologist, psychologist, schoolteacher, hairstylist, day-care worker, social worker, personnel manager, bartender, and mental health counselor. Leisure activities that Social people enjoy include sports of all kinds (either as spectator or participant), community service, social clubs, shopping, gourmet cooking, volunteer service in hospitals and retirement homes, and community education programs.

Enterprising-Persuasive

Enterprising-Persuasive people like to manipulate or train others for economic gain or organizational success. They usually are outgoing, self-confident, and persuasive. They use interpersonal skills and abilities to persuade other people. Enterprising-Persuasive personalities are often leaders in a wide variety of settings. Their leadership is not behind the scene; rather, it is openly persuading and encouraging the efforts of others.

Others describe the Enterprising-Persuasive person as a good friend or leader who is optimistic, self-confident, energetic, ambitious, verbally skilled, and sociable. This person typically is also cheerful, adventurous, somewhat impulsive, and playful. Enterprising-Persuasive people are least like Investigative-Scientific types.

Occupations that Enterprising-Persuasive people tend to enjoy include building contractor, business executive, car salesperson, head coach, insurance salesperson, funeral director, retail store manager, barber, politician, hotel clerk, merchandise buyer, travel guide, real estate salesperson, and golf or sports club manager. Nonvocational activities that Enterprising-Persuasive people get pleasure from include shopping, entering contests, adventure sports and activities, researching genealogy, collecting political memorabilia, and playing games of chance.

Conventional-Informational

The Conventional-Informational person prefers activities that involve keeping records, organizing written and numerical information, and working with information technology and computers in order to achieve organizational or personal goals. Conventional-Informational people tend to be predictable—sticking to traditional, tried-and-true ways of doing things. They use their intellectual and organizational abilities to solve problems at work, home, and in other settings.

Friends, family or co-workers describe the Conventional-Informational person as orderly, conscientious, informing, practical, persistent, and conscientious. This person is very reliable—someone who can be counted on to complete tasks. Conventional-Informational people like quality and want to ensure quality performance or products. Typically, they are least like Artistic-Creative people.

Occupations or professions suited to Conventional-Informational personalities include doing things related to business detail or keeping records or doing computations in such work as computer programmer, office clerk, traffic clerk, medical records processor, editorial assistant, secretary, ticket agent, accountant, postal inspector, banker, and investment analyst. Enjoyable leisure activities include collecting all sorts of things, playing card games, and playing computer games.

Personality in Action

Individually, you and your spouse should reread and think about the descriptions of the six personality types. Which type best describes you? Perhaps two or three of the six types describe you. Consider your interests. Using the list below, rank the six types, with 1 being most like you and 6 being least like you.

_____Realistic-Practical

_____Investigative-Scientific

_____Artistic-Creative

_____Social-Nurturing

_____Enterprising-Persuasive

_____Conventional-Informational

Now take turns explaining your rankings to each other. In your discussion, use specific examples. For example, Dale described himself as principally Investigative-Scientific. However, he also saw many of the Realistic-Practical characteristics in himself. Growing up, Dale was a good student who went on to medical school and became a surgeon. This is the Investigative-Scientific aspect of his personality which he ranked #1. In his spare time, he enjoys the outdoors and likes to work in the yard with his wife, Deanna. He is a volunteer assistant Scoutmaster who works with young men and takes them on a number of outdoor camping trips during the year. One of his sons is in his scout troop, which helps Dale justify the time spent in this volunteer service. This is the Realistic-Practical component of his personality which he ranked #2.

Deanna described herself as primarily Enterprising-Persuasive. She has a college degree in public relations and worked for a number of years for a small company directing their marketing efforts. When the first of their three children came along, Deanna and Dale decided that she would be a stay-at-home mom, which they both wanted for each other and their family. This is the Social-Nurturing aspect of her personality which she ranked #2.

Next, explain to each other how you see each other according to the six types. Again, as you discuss this, use specific examples. As they talked, Deanna and Dale realized that they were on the same page in describing one another.

Discuss how you would describe your marriage according to the six categories. Take into account your individual and shared activities (work and volunteer service) and your leisure-time interests and activities. Try to identify your individual and collective interests and activities so that you might describe your marriage according to the six types. For example, in their discussion, Dale and Deanna found that one or two categories did not adequately describe their marriage. They determined that really their marriage encompassed three or four of the six types. First, they identified their marriage as being primarily Social-Nurturing because of their roles as parents and as spouses. When they married, they committed to focus on and support the child-rearing stage of their lives. They identified the Realistic-Conventional type as the second most significant aspect of their marriage and family life, which centers on being together outdoors and engaging in physical activity as much as possible. They also believe that they are practical and traditional in many of their values, and while they interact with other family members and friends, they prefer to do things together as a family. The Investigative-Scientific type ranked third because Dale and Deanna value education and understanding the world around them. They also enjoy participating in local cultural and civic activities as a couple, so they ranked the Artistic-Creative type fourth in their marriage.

Conclusion

Our goal in this chapter was to introduce you to a method of classifying your individual personalities. We also invited you to use the six hexagonal types as a means for discussing your similarities and differences as marriage partners. Then we encouraged you to use this information to identify your marital personality so that you might better understand the dynamics of your relationship. We hope this information and process will enable you to develop a means and a language for planning and achieving many of your marital and individual goals.

CHAPTER 13
The Dynamics of Birth Order

THE KEY: Understanding the birth order or sibling position in your and your spouse's family of origin can be useful in understanding your interactions as husband and wife.

A couple's families of origin—that is, the families in which they grew up—have a tremendous impact on who each spouse is. The husband's and wife's families exposed them to different life events, values, traditions, and practices as they grew up.

The order in which each spouse is born or adopted into his or her nuclear family is termed *birth order* or *sibling position*. Birth order often plays an important role in the formation of the personality and the way a person interacts with others. Parents do not intentionally treat each child differently because of birth order, but the dynamics of the changing, growing family mean that children in different birth-order positions are treated differently.

The Family System

A family is much more than just a collection of individuals who do their own thing and go their own way. In a family, everyone is affected by everyone else. The ways family members affect one another are typically subtle and not necessarily planned. For example, if someone in the family gets sick, the others must adjust in some ways. Often, Mom adjusts more than anyone else. When a new child comes into the family, each family member adapts to his or her new position in the family. The addition of each new family member makes interaction among all family members more complex. Adaptation is necessary and normal in order for the family to care for all family members. This adaptation occurs whether the child is born into or adopted into the family.

Another way to look at the idea of the family system and birth order is to hypothesize that every child needs and desires to belong to a family. In addition, each child needs to fulfill a unique role and to contribute to the dynamics of the family.

Try to recall the roles that family members played in your family of origin. Perhaps one child was labeled or thought of as the "black sheep" of the family, the one who refused to do what the parents wanted. Another might have been just the opposite, the one who tried hard to please the parents, the "perfect child" or "favorite." One child may have been the clown, always making jokes in order to decrease tension among family members. Typically, some of these childhood roles are carried into marriage.

For example, growing up, Sammy was the jokester and fun-loving child in his family. When things got tense among his siblings or between Mom and Dad, Sammy always injected some humor or distracting funny event. In fact, one of the things that his wife, Sally, enjoyed about him during courtship was that Sammy was such a fun-loving and easygoing guy. In their marriage, when things get rough between him and Sally, Sammy tends to make jokes about the situation.

While at times that can be helpful and appropriate, sometimes it also can interfere with the couple's ability to have a serious discussion in order to solve a problem.

Birth Order

Although many factors influence who we become, the roles that family members learn from birth order or sibling position partially influence their personality characteristics, behaviors, and interactions with others. Reports claim that as early as 1874, Sir Francis Galton observed an unusually large number of only children or firstborn children among British scientists. He concluded that parents treated first (or only) children differently than later children. In the early 1900s, psychotherapist Dr. Alfred Adler wrote that the order in which individuals are born into a family shapes their personalities in important ways. He pointed out that firstborn children generally share common characteristics, as do middleborn children and youngest children. The same is true of only children—those with no brothers or sisters.

Birth order determines the way that parents respond to their children and the ways that children react to older and younger siblings. From a family systems point of view, each child fulfills different needs in family dynamics and interaction. Adults carry the influence of birth order into their marriage and other aspects of their lives. This influence is particularly noticeable in interactions between spouses and other family members.

Talking as a couple about birth order can be useful and fun. Answering the questions below will help direct your discussion as you read the rest of this chapter. Separately, you and your spouse should write down brief responses to the questions. Then set aside some time to talk about your answers before you continue reading. Recall that birth order categories include only child, oldest child, middle child or children, and youngest child.

- Where are you in your family's birth order?
- What was it like for you in your family of origin?
- List some characteristics, adjectives, or phrases that describe your role(s) in your family of origin.
- List some characteristics, adjectives, or phrases that describe your personality traits in your family as you grew up.
- What characteristics make someone of your birth order a good spouse?
- What cautions or suggestions do you have for a spouse married to someone of your birth order?

How did it go? Perhaps this exercise gave you some insight into both you and your spouse's family of origin and how that shaped you as people. Perhaps you now have some additional clues as to why you are such an excellent spouse!

Birth Order Characteristics

As you read and discuss the information below, keep the following ideas in mind.

- The birth order descriptions are generalizations. While such generalizations are often true and have implications for you, the psychological experience and climate varies within each family.
- Generally speaking, if three years or more separate siblings, the differences among the children may not be as pronounced.
- Twins have their own birth order, just as other siblings. One

twin is older and one twin is younger, even if they are born just minutes apart. While twins are often considered the same age, the birth order influences each child in subtle ways.

- Sometimes birth orders are interchanged. For example, a firstborn and secondborn in one family may show characteristics that are opposite of a firstborn and secondborn in another family.
- The primary goal of studying birth order is to understand interpersonal dynamics, not to predict behavior.

The Only Child

The only child, or firstborn child, provides an example of the importance of the family environment in the child's life. The way that a child comes to a couple can have a powerful impact on the way they treat that child. For example, if a couple's only child is a "miracle,"—perhaps long-awaited or born after a high-risk pregnancy—and the couple had wanted to have other children, this child may be treated much differently than a child who is an "oops" and was not planned or even wanted. In the first instance, the child may receive his parents' undivided attention and may be overprotected and treated as very special. In the second instance, the unwanted child may not be cared for or nurtured properly and may be emotionally neglected.

If an only child is wanted and valued and appropriately nurtured by parents—a mother and father living in the same home—the child generally becomes skilled at relating to adults. Only children tend to be conscientious and reliable and often are remarkably socially mature for their chronological age. They tend to follow their parents wishes and are often very compliant. Only children tend to be good students and achievers.

In marriage, many of these traits carry over and are very desirable. Only children tend to be loyal and good providers. On the other hand, an only child has had little or no experience living with someone his own age and may seem uncooperative and selfish. Only children may be very critical of themselves and others and sometimes hold unrealistic expectations. Again, this can be a positive or negative characteristic in marriage.

The Firstborn

Oldest or firstborn children are usually center stage in the family. The oldest child is an experiment for the parents. Everything she does is a "first" for her parents. They focus on firsts—the first smile, first coo, first time sitting up and crawling, first steps, first words, and so on. All of these behaviors and milestones are usually met with delighted approval from parents, grandparents, aunts, and uncles.

The oldest child's role in the family is to do those things that win the family's approval. Early on, before other children come along, that approval comes from the parents. Later, that approval may be from siblings as well as other adults and important people in the firstborn's life. Firstborns are high achievers and, like only children, tend to be responsible and productive.

In marriage and other interpersonal situations, firstborns demonstrate many positive characteristics. They tend to be good planners and are well organized, reliable, and conscientious. Often they are very serious, although they may have an underlying dry sense of humor. Firstborns like to be in control and in charge; they tend to be leaders.

How might these characteristics play out in marriage? A firstborn spouse may insist on being in charge. She may be too work-oriented, a perfectionist, someone who is not spontaneous or thoughtful. The firstborn probably prefers to spend time with her spouse and children as opposed to friends or coworkers. Firstborns are wonderful problem solvers and tend to take on as much responsibility in the marriage as a spouse is willing to give.

The Middle Child/Middle Children

Middle children are "sandwiched" between the oldest and youngest. That is, whether one child or many occupy the middle position in the family birth order, they are always out of sight between the oldest and the youngest. Middle children may feel squeezed out of a position of importance and feel rather insignificant compared to their siblings.

Middle children are pulled and pushed in many directions. Middle children generally don't like confrontation, although they are good compromisers. They sometimes feel inferior to others and tend to be easily embarrassed. Thus, they are often quiet and tend to hide their feelings. Middleborns tend to like choices rather than just one option.

The oldest middle child—that is, the second child in a family of four or more children—tends toward behavior that is the opposite of his older sibling. He may seem rebellious or uncooperative compared to the oldest child who busily fulfills her role to meet family and parental expectations.

Middleborns tend to be good negotiators and compromisers. They tend to have many friends and stable relationships. They are often the peacemakers in the family and in other close relationships. As an adult, a middle child often contributes significantly to a stable and satisfactory marriage. Middle children are often partners in happy and long-lasting marriages.

Years ago the following poem was published in a newspaper. This poem wonderfully and insightfully describes the benefits of marrying a middleborn. Notice that the author is unknown. Perhaps he or she was one of those anonymous and ambiguous middle children!

Middle Children
Middle children are used to giving in to the younger and the older.
Middle children are used to turning soft, mild cheeks to the child who's older.
Middle children make cheer their talent, smiling even through hand-me-down downings.
Middle children will play a willing audience for the other's clownings.
Middle children are open-hearted.
Middle children will fetch and carry.
Middle children don't need unspoiling.
Middle children are nice to marry.
—Author Unknown

The Youngest Child

Dr. Kevin Leman, a noted author on birth order, is reported to have said something to the effect that if you're going to have a party and want everyone to enjoy a good time, you'd be wise to invite several youngest children. These are the fun-loving, good-time folks.

As the youngest in the family, this child has many mothers and fathers. When Mom and Dad are tired of parenting, older siblings take over. Older children formally and informally educate and train the youngest child throughout his life.

The family pecking order often turns lastborns into great observers of family and interpersonal dynamics. They often are good listeners whom others share their problems with or confide in. The youngest child has seen it all and tends to be easygoing and tolerant. He can understand another's point of view, whether or not he agrees with it. Lastborns value harmony in family relationships, which usually is helpful in marriage. While they are sensitive and can have their feelings hurt quite easily, they tend to get over hurtful statements and actions faster than their older siblings.

While the lastborn is frequently told what to do, he is also skilled at getting his own way. On the downside, the youngest can be somewhat irresponsible and disorganized. Often, lastborns have been coddled, and thus are not used to major responsibility. They can be self-centered because they have been given a lot of attention and often many material things and privileges that their older siblings did not receive.

Your Birth Order in Your Marriage

Marriage is an intimate relationship in which two individuals can become one in purpose as they spend their lives together. Living together and carving out a future together is one of the great rewards of being a married couple. With that reward in mind, consider the impact of birth order for you as a married couple.

Let's review the questions you discussed at the beginning of this chapter.

- Where are you in your family's birth order?
- What was it like for you in your family? As the two of you have thought about and discussed this question, perhaps you have gained a new sensitivity, appreciation, and understanding of

the dynamics between you and your parents and siblings. Couples frequently report that after their dialogue about this question, they not only understand their families of origin better, but they also are better able to articulate their specific goals and desires for their marriage and for their roles as parents.

• List some characteristics, adjectives, or phrases that describe your personality in your family as you grew up. Now let's add to that. List and discuss some of the characteristics that describe your personality and your roles in your marriage. Try to identify the characteristics that operate in your marriage today that relate to your birth order. Talk to each other—not just about your own characteristics, but also about those you see in your spouse. Describe your spouse's personality and his roles in your marriage today.

• What characteristics make someone of your birth order a good spouse? This should be easy and fun! It is okay to brag as you discuss your good characteristics. Tell your spouse what characteristics from her birth order make her a good spouse for you.

• What cautions or suggestions do you have for a spouse married to someone of your birth order? First, try to identify the characteristics that might be challenging. For example, if you are firstborn, you might struggle with perfectionism, or stubbornness, or bossiness. As a middleborn, you might tend to hide your feelings, even in your relationship with your spouse. As a lastborn, perhaps you are somewhat disorganized and irresponsible, or maybe you're self-centered. Now, how can you and your spouse begin changing your negative behaviors? Discussing these issues will increase the caring, trust, and respect that you have for each other.

Your Children's Birth Order and Your Marriage

Consider these questions: What influence do you hope to have, or are you having, on your children? What are you hoping for, or what have you experienced in regard to the impact of your children on you and your marriage? Even though birth order occurs and primarily affects children, family relationships are reciprocal, meaning that the birth order and characteristics of children also impact parents. Take time to discuss the influence of your children's birth order and personalities on your marital relationship.

CHAPTER 14
Creating a Nurturing Marriage

THE KEY: Creating and maintaining a nurturing and positive marriage is a key to a great marriage.

Link, Connect, Bond, Relate, Associate, Tie, Join

It has been said that "no person is an island." From a family-relations point of view, this means that no person truly lives alone, that everyone is connected to at least one other person through a familial or other relationship. For some, the connection is primarily physical; that is, the relationship meets basic needs for survival. For others, the relationship might meet emotional needs. And for still others it might be a spiritual or other meaningful relationship.

Certainly, spouses do not marry to be alone. Marriage creates a relationship in which the wife and husband form a unique and intimate bond with a special kind of sharing and connection. This is a reason for marriage. This is the reason that marriage is good for the spouses, or *nurturing*, in all sorts of ways—physical, emotional, spiritual, financial, and so forth.

Marriage Dynamics

Years ago a pioneering family therapist, Virginia Satir, observed some common dynamics in families. Her observations related primarily to relationships between parents and children and even beyond that to relationships with grandparents, aunts and uncles, and other family members. Satir's observations are also useful as we look at the relationship between wives and husbands.

When assessing your marriage, you can observe at least four aspects that build the nurturing foundation of your relationship:

1. The self-worth or self-esteem of each spouse
2. The communication between spouses
3. The rules or expectations that guide the marriage
4. The way the married couple relates to others outside their marriage

Self-Esteem

Much has been written about self-esteem, which is how an individual feels about himself or herself. A person's self-esteem is directly and indirectly influenced by others. A person who is continually belittled or demeaned by others is not likely not to think well of himself or herself. Similarly, a person who lives in a punishing environment is likely to be unhappy, perhaps unproductive, and not much fun. We say that this person has a low self-esteem; the punishing and non-rewarding personal interaction has contributed to this person's unhappiness and low self-esteem. On the other hand, a person who is esteemed or treated well by others is likely to think well of themselves. Such a person will have a belief that they are worthwhile, resulting in a positive self-esteem.

Communication

Much has been written about communication, and we have discussed that in other chapters. Almost all healthy marriages have good communication skills between the husband and wife. As noted elsewhere, research has shown that both marriage counselors and couples seeking marriage counseling indicate that poor communication is the most frequent problem presented in marriage counseling. Couples who perceive problems tend to want to improve their communication as a means to have a more satisfying and successful marital relationship.

RULES AND EXPECTATIONS

Every marriage is guided by rules and expectations. Very few of these rules are written, although many are discussed as the couple creates their marriage. You learned rules regarding your role as a husband or wife by watching your parents' (or significant others') marriage. One of the tasks for you as couple, then, has been to take those rules and expectations from your life experience and previous learning and apply them as a framework for your marriage. Of course, you and your spouse will be challenged as you negotiate and adapt your previous learning to your marriage!

RELATIONSHIPS WITH OTHERS

As we explained earlier, no marriage can function well in isolation. There really are no hermit marriages. In today's world, couples do not live alone; they relate to other people around them. Certainly, some people are much less social than others, but all couples relate to other people in order to live and function in society.

Troubled Marriages

Let's discuss the contrast between troubled marriages and nurturing marriages. Sometimes you will hear the term *dysfunctional* used as a synonym for a troubled marriage. Similarly, the term *functional* is used as a synonym for a nurturing marriage. If such language conveys to you a better understanding of what we are attempting to discuss, so be it. Note, however, that most of us are somewhat troubled at times, or perhaps dysfunctional. Similarly, we are nurturing and nurtured at other times, hopefully most of the time!

In troubled marriages, the self-worth or self-esteem of one or both of the partners generally is low. That is, either the wife or the husband (or both) does not feel very good about him- or herself. The reasons for this can be many. Perhaps one spouse came from a troubled family or has been mistreated in other relationships. Perhaps one spouse's work environment is hostile or negative. In some instances, people marry as a means of overcoming low self-esteem. The couple may have believed that marriage would somehow be therapeutic, or be the means for the person with low self-esteem to become whole. This is not usually how things work out.

In troubled marriages, we often find that the communication between the spouses is poor. You may think that communication between spouses is generally good; otherwise they would not have married. But, sadly, this is not always the case. Sometimes, couples with good overall communication let certain issues eat away at or destroy their relationship. Such issues as finances, family-of-origin troubles, in-laws, parenting practices, and sexual problems, if not resolved, can lead to marital disharmony. In troubled marriages, communication may not really be honest, and may even be deceitful. Often, spouses' communication is vague or indirect, which can lead to marital disharmony.

All marriages have and continue to develop rules and expectations.

In troubled marriages, rules and expectations tend to be rigid or non-negotiable. That is, partners lack the ability to be flexible and to adapt to new situations. We all know that marriage introduces many new situations for both the wife and husband! Sometimes the rigidity is learned from one's family of origin: one partner's thoughts or actions match the way his or her parents did things in their marriage; therefore, believes this partner, that is the way things should be done in this marriage. Keep in mind that this probably is not intentional. Numerous studies and practical experience show that behavior in marriage is learned directly and indirectly from one's family of origin. If behavior is learned, then new ways of thinking and behaving can be learned!

In troubled marriages, the ways that the married couple relates to others outside their marriage is often blaming and/or fearful. Virginia Satir referred to this as the "link to society." In this type of relationship, spouses tend to dwell on the negative things that happen to them, so they perceive their frustrated or failed marriage, family, or even society as someone else's fault. Sadly, these individuals' marriages often end in divorce because they blame marriage difficulties on their spouse—"it was her/his fault." Or they may see their bankruptcy or other business or personal failure as someone else's fault, always looking for someone else to blame for life events.

Nurturing Marriages

In nurturing marriages, the self-worth or self-esteem of both spouses is moderate to high, but neither spouse is cocky or overconfident. They recognize and appreciate their talents and strengths while also are aware of their weaknesses. Both partners feel good about themselves. They feel good about their relationship and would rate their marriage as satisfactory to very satisfactory and stable. Each spouse has had a relatively happy childhood and good experiences in relationships before the marriage. If they haven't had the best of childhoods, or relationship history, they have worked very hard to have positive esteem and healthy expectations of themselves and relationships. As a couple and as individuals, these people are seen by others as confident and competent, as well as generally pleasing to be around.

In the nurturing marriage, typically the communication between the spouses is good. They are honest and open in their communication. They do not manipulate each other. Spouses are constantly aware of their communication with one another and strive to improve it. In other words, they value communication as a part of their relationship and strive to keep it working well for them. Because of their good communication, these couples are able to deal with issues that confront them such as finances, family-of-origin troubles, in-laws, parenting, and sexual concerns.

In a nurturing marriage, the rules and expectations that guide the couple are appropriately flexible and negotiable. It is true that discovering and appropriately modifying rules and expectations is a lifelong effort in a satisfactory marriage. If we observed a nurturing couple, we would find that this is obvious from their interaction. They care about one another, and this caring is demonstrated in the ways that they treat one another and try to understand each other. They probably have fun recalling the rules or traditions in their families of origin, and they discuss how those traditions might be, or not be, a part of their marriage.

In nurturing marriages, the couple's link to society, or the ways spouses relate to others outside their marriage, is hopeful and open. They are involved with others outside their marriage in positive ways. These couples face as many challenges as troubled couples, but they affiliate with others rather than isolating themselves from others. This attitude helps them learn from others as well as give and receive emotional and psychological support. These reciprocal relationships tend to help people maintain a healthy and adaptable emotional and psychological state. Here, the spouses relate to others in their roles as a married couple, which tends to reinforce and support the value of their marriage relationship in practical ways.

Evaluate Your Marriage

As you discuss the topic of connecting or relating to others outside your marriage, consider some important points. First, in some ways there are no right or wrong ways to relate. The main criteria is that a couple's behavior works for them and that it does not infringe upon or impede other people, such as their children. If these criteria are met, then it is probably appropriate for that couple.

The following questions can assist you as you evaluate ways you and your spouse nurture one another are you relate to each other and also to others outside the marriage.

First, every person has feelings of self-worth or self-esteem that are either primarily positive or primarily negative. What are they for you? What are they for your spouse? What helps you have a feeling of self-worth? What are the positive things that you do or that your spouse does that make you both feel good about yourselves as individuals? What are the negative things that you do to yourself or to your spouse that may cause low self-esteem? If you can identify these positive and negative behaviors in your relationship, you can then strengthen them or correct them. Remember, the greatest resource a married person has for nurturing is their spouse. Similarly, the greatest resource a married person has to assist in correcting or improving a behavior and one's attitude is a loving spouse.

This same idea of self-esteem can relate to you as a couple. What is your couple esteem or marriage esteem? How do you see yourselves as a married couple? Do you feel good about your marriage? Do you value, or esteem, your marriage? Why or why not? What are the positive things about your marriage relationship? Take time to discuss them together. If you see areas of concern, discuss them and think of ways that you might improve your marriage esteem and couple esteem.

Specific Tips to Increase Esteem

Set a specific goal for every day and achieve it. It doesn't have to be a big thing. It could be as simple as, "I am going to compliment my sweetheart (or yourself) 10 times today," or doing something nice for someone else without any expectations in return (i.e., "no strings attached").

Second, both you and your spouse communicate with each other. How is your communication? What happens as a result of your communication? In a marriage relationship, *it is impossible not to communicate.* Silence communicates something, doesn't it? Certainly verbal statements communicate. In what ways do you wish to improve your communication? In what ways is your communication satisfactory?

Specific Tips to Improve Communication

Remember to LUV your spouse. See chapter 6 for a much more in-depth discussion on improving communication.

Third, every couple follows rules. A synonym for rules is

expectations. What are some of the rules in your marriage? How well do these rules or expectations work for you and your spouse? We have found that in marriage counseling, a useful question to ask a couple is, "What are the rules in your marriage?" Often the couple looks at the counselor and then each other before one begins with something like, "Oh, you mean I make the money and she spends it?" Or one might say, "No one sits in dad's recliner," or "Mom rules the kitchen." These are rules or expectations that guide marriage and family life. Undoubtedly, you as a married couple have developed rules for your relationship. Discuss together what these rules might be and how they influence you and your marital interaction? Typically, roles that spouses play in the marriage are the implicit and explicit rules that guide the marriage. Discuss together and write down the primary rules and expectations that guide your marriage. You may also find it interesting to look back on your parents' marriage and identify some of the major rules or expectations of your family as you were growing up.

Specific Suggestions for Effective Rules

Revisiting chapter 3 will help you identify further expectations (rules) you have for yourself and spouse. Be adaptable! Have a rule in your marriage that allows you to change some rules! You are two unique individuals that will continue to grow and change in many ways as you age. Children will grow and change. Situations change. The couples that experience a nurturing marriage use their rights to modify rules (expectations) as they need. Fourth, every married couple relates to others outside of their marriage relationship. How do you as a couple relate to others outside of your marriage? What are the results of the way in which you relate or communicate with them?

Are you hopeful and open in your relationship with others, or are you blaming and fearful? Consider how you as individuals and as a couple relate to the following:

- Your family of origin; that is, your parents, siblings, in-laws, cousins, aunts and uncles, grandparents, and so forth
- Your children
- Your neighbors
- Your community
- Your church
- Your local, state, and national government
- Your heritage

Specific Suggestions to Improve your Social Connections

Which of the list above could help strengthen your relationship? What has gotten in your way in the past of connecting with these individuals/organizations? What would be the first step for you to take to connect? The second? Third?

Remember that you and your sweetheart have the ability to create a nurturing marriage. Consider the ways that you influence each other's self-esteem, the ways that you communicate, the rules that guide your marriage, and the way that you as a couple relate to others outside of your marriage. Then, continue to create the marriage of your dreams.

CHAPTER 15

Looking Deeper at Your Family of Origin

THE KEY: In great marriages, spouses understand how their family relationships while growing up can influence their present and future.

Who am I? It's just a simple question, three simple words. It is an easy question to ask, yet it takes tremendous courage and strength to attempt to answer. In marriage, not only do you get to try to answer "Who am I," but you get to answer another three-word question, "Who are we?"

One overly simple answer to the first question is the following. You are the sum total of your genetics and experiences, and all of the actions, thoughts, emotions, beliefs, and ideas that you have ever had. That still really doesn't answer the first question does it? At least it doesn't answer it in any meaningful way. The reason it isn't meaningful is that it doesn't describe any of the specifics. If you could write every one of those things out, you would start to get a *glimpse* of who you are.

What most people don't realize is that you and your spouse are the outcome of thousands upon thousands of people who came before, each with their own genetics, experiences, actions, thoughts, and so on. Another thing many people don't realize is that you and your sweetheart are also the beginning, the headwaters, of thousands upon thousands of people who will come directly from you. If you were looking at a map of your genealogy and were able to see your descendants along with your ancestors, it would look something like the picture below. In this context it is difficult to say that one life can't make a difference, or doesn't matter. You absolutely do matter and can make a difference.

It is also difficult to say in this context that you aren't influenced by anyone else! This chapter will help you find out how you have inherited more than just genetics from your parents and grandparents. This inheritance has already profoundly impacted your marriage and will continue to impact it.

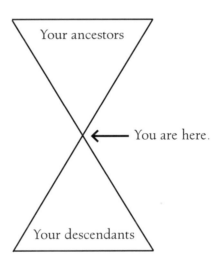

Your ancestors

You are here.

Your descendants

Family of Origin

Some of you may be saying, "I will make sure that my family is nothing like the family I grew up in." Fair enough—you will probably do your best to make that happen. But if it wasn't for the family you grew up in, how would you have known what you *don't* want? We would submit that even when you do the opposite of what you've experienced, your decisions are still being impacted by your family of origin. You're still using what happened in the family you grew up in as the measuring stick to make decisions in your present family and marriage.

It certainly is an appropriate thing that you want to change some negative patterns that you perceived when growing up within your family of origin. Yet one of the dangers of using emotionally or physically difficult experiences as a comparison for how well you are currently doing is that you may still be missing the mark. Let's pretend that you grew up with parents whom you saw as "controlling." They made every decision for you. If you didn't comply, you were severely punished.

You get married and resolve to "not be like your parents" and you try to give your children maximum freedom. When they reach adolescence they want to make all their decisions themselves—doing what they want, when they want. You find yourself without any influence at all with these children. All your kids have to say for you to back off is, "You're so much like grandma," or "You're so much like grandpa," or "You just want to control my life." Your fear of being "controlling" may have kept you from setting and maintaining *appropriate* boundaries.

The same is true about your adult romantic relationships. If you keep using your past relationships as the comparison to determine the quality of your current relationship, you may be missing important aspects of marriage. Education on what constitutes a great marriage can be helpful to stay out of this trap. With a more stable benchmark, you then can evaluate your marriage on criteria that is more reliable than "what you don't want to repeat."

Having a good understanding of what your experiences have been is incredibly helpful. The caution remains about using your past to determine the quality of your present relationship. But by understanding where you have come from, you can gain added insight into *why* you do some of the things you do. These things include:

1. Why you married your sweetheart
2. Your ideas of what a good husband is
3. Your ideas of what a good wife is
4. How your values about things like sex, money, and parenting developed
5. How problems are solved
6. What it means to be loved
7. How to show love

Diagramming Your Family Map

You are going to make a family tree of sorts. You are going to be the expert for your side of the family on this page. Your sweetheart should make a separate page for his or her side of the family following this same process.

The first thing that you need to do is get a large piece of paper, at least 8.5 X 11. Lay the paper horizontally on a table or desk. Then draw a circle (if you are a woman) or a square (if you are a man) at the bottom center of the page. Draw another square or circle for you spouse an inch or so away. Draw a line connecting the two of you together. That shows that you are married. On your page, you are going to show your parents, and both sets of grandparents.

Your paper will look something like this:

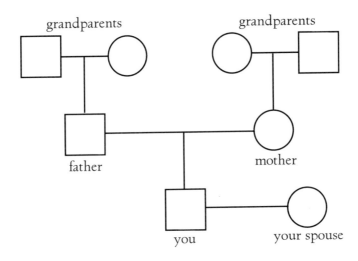

Write everyone's name and current age in the appropriate circle or square. Again, women are represented by circles and men are represented by squares. If an individual has passed away, put an "x" through the shape but write his or her name, the age at which he or she died, and the cause of death. If you, or anyone else on the chart, have had more than one marriage, simply add another circle or square next to that person. Put two slashes through the connecting line to represent a divorce. For example, say your father had been married previously. You would put a circle to the *left* of his square with a line connecting the two together and draw two slashes (//) through the line to represent the divorce.

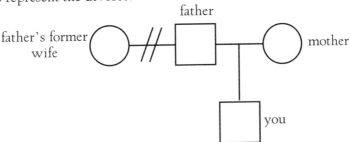

In today's era of adoptions, marriages, divorces, and remarriages, these charts can get a bit complicated. If you need to simplify some, you can do the following. Keep all previous marriages (if any) that you and your sweetheart have had. At the parent level, make sure you record those persons who have had the most influence in your life. By influence, we mean anyone who you believe has impacted *your* life for better or worse. At the grandparent level, put any spouse who was a major influence on your *parent's* life.

Now that you have the people listed, here comes the fun part. If you don't know the answers to some of these questions, ask someone who might know. This is especially true when it comes to answering questions about your grandparents and their marriages. Don't forget to put down information about yourself and your own relationship!

Individual Attributes and Comparisons

Next to each *person*, list a few words (up to 10) that describe their strengths and weaknesses. Do this for yourself as well. Examples of strengths might be things such as kind, caring, generous, sense of humor, fun, thoughtful, intelligent, and so on. Examples of weaknesses could be temper, physically violent, sharp tongue, alcoholic, overly shy, codependent, passive, aloof, and so on.

Now answer the following questions:

1. How are you similar to your same-gender parent and grandparents? What strengths and weaknesses do you have that they may have had?

2. How are you different from your same-gender parent and grandparents?

3. Have you developed any traits—either strengths or weaknesses—

that were the opposite of your parents?

4. How is your spouse similar to your *opposite-gendered* parent? So, if you are the husband , how is your wife similar to your mother? Be honest!

5. How is your spouse different from your *opposite-gendered* parent? Be honest! Are any of those differences extreme? For example, say your father was verbally aggressive and demeaning. Is your husband reserved and overly complimentary?

6. How similar is your mom to your dad's mother? How are they different?

7. How similar is your father to your mom's father? How are they different?

Before you move on to examining the relationships in your current family, it is important to understand the difference between *what* and *how*.

- *What* refers to the specific interests, employment, hobbies, or activities that occur with individuals that impact their relationships with others.
- *How* refers to the actual interaction process, that goes on between partners.

For example, Grandpa Joe spent an enormous amount of time away from his wife and marriage to pursue his interest of fishing. Likewise, you may spend an enormous amount of time away from your wife and marriage pursuing photography. When someone accuses you of being just like Grandpa Joe, you adamantly say, "I'm nothing like him! He fished, I don't fish at all." You would be being caught up in the *what* of the situation. The *function*, the *how*, is no different. You and Grandpa Joe both spent a lot of time outside the marriage pursuing your personal interests.

Another example may be that your mother frequently would bring up financial problems to your dad. She would pursue him, literally, around the house and finally get to the point of yelling at him. Once she got to this point, Dad would listen. You would be repeating your parents marital interaction if you are the one constantly bringing up issues to discuss in the relationship and eventually "loose it" before your husband listens. Your marital dance, your *how*, is similar to your parents, although you may or may not have problems with finances.

So, as you read through these next sections, be sure to focus on *how* rather than *what*. There may be patterns that you are repeating in terms of *how* that do not relate to the *whats*. (It's possible that there are patterns you are also repeating in terms of *what*, and this is good to be aware of as well.) If you are having a difficult time finding patterns, it is a strong possibility you are getting caught up on the *whats* more than the *hows*.

Marital Relationships

- On each *marital link* of the diagram that you drew, put down how many years the couple was or has been married. Don't forget your own relationship.
- What are/were the marital strengths?
- What are/were the marital weaknesses?
- Rate each relationship on a scale of 1 to 10 on the following attributes (10 being very strong on the attribute and 1 meaning they really struggled with it):
  - Friendship with each other
  - Commitment to marriage
  - Loyalty to their partner as a person

- Adaptable or flexible
- Problem solving
- Understanding each other
- How long did the dating process take with each relationship before the wedding?
- Who proposed to whom? (You could draw an engagement ring beside the proposer.)
- Who was employed outside the home? (You could write the word "paycheck" next to those who worked outside the home.)
- Who took charge of work around the home? (Draw a broom next to this person.)
- Who brought up issues or problems that needed to be solved?
- Put a "$" by the person who managed the money in the relationship.
- Put an "*" by the person who had the final say on the *major* decisions?
- Who disciplined the children most? How did they do it?
- What traditions did each relationship have?
- Of course if any of the decisions discussed here were equally made, indicate that.

Parent-Child Relationships

For each of the following questions, answer on a scale of 1 to 10 (10 means you got along great; 1 means that you had a very distant and/or rocky relationship; 5 means that the relationship is/was somewhere in the middle). Write your answer on the paper. If you want, you can write your answer next to an arrow or dashed line connecting the two people in the relationship you have been asked about.

- How well do/did you get along with your father?
- How well do/did you get along with your mother?
- How well do/did you get along with your father-in-law?
- How well do/did you get along with your mother-in-law?
- How well do/did your mother get along with *her* father?
- How well do/did your mother get along with *her* mother?
- How well do/did your mother get along with her father-in-law?
- How well do/did your mother get along with her mother-in-law?
- How well do/did your father get along with *his* father?
- How well do/did your father get along with *his* mother?
- How well do/did your father get along with his father-in-law?
- How well do/did your father get along with his mother-in-law?

Finding Patterns

Now that you have sufficiently analyzed and rated yourself and your family history, it is time to see if your relationship with your sweetheart has followed any patterns that have been passed down from your family of origin. You may have seen some patterns, individual characteristics, and similarities (or opposites) on your family tree. Looking at your sweetheart's family map, how do you fit in with that family background?

- Looking at you and your partner's page of information, whose marriage does your marriage most resemble? In what ways is it similar?
- What strengths does your marriage have that previous marriages in your families have also had?
- What strengths does your marriage have that previous marriages

haven not had?

• What weaknesses does your marriage have that previous marriages in your families have also had?

• What weaknesses does your marriage have that previous marriages *have not* had?

What Do I Do with All This Information?

As your awareness of yourself and relationship increases, the number of positive directions you can go from here also increases. Make a list of some of your personal and relational weaknesses and strengths. Looking at your family tree, you can now see why you have some of the strengths and weaknesses you do have. You may also see more reasons why you were attracted to your sweetheart. Your spouse may have many characteristics (or opposite characteristics) of your parents and grandparents.

Now that you have identified some weaknesses, the next step is to think about a goal that would eliminate a weakness or turn it into a strength. You can turn to chapter 21, "Using 'What's the DIF' to Understand Growth and Change in Your Relationship," to get more details on charting growth change. In summary, it is most effective to identify what you *want* when trying to make changes rather than simply knowing what you don't want. Taking a marriage enrichment course, reading a book, or talking to a professional marriage therapist are all great ways to help you identify some specific goals to work toward.

There is an important difference between "avoiding the mistakes of the past" and working toward a specific, action-oriented goal. Avoidance-oriented goals promote a mind-set in which you are constantly looking for evidence that "things are getting bad." Working toward specific, action-oriented goals will give you a mind-set in which you will look for evidence to support your positive efforts.

As you are working toward reversing some trends in your marriage, remember the strengths that you each have individually and the strengths you gain from your marriage together. It will be those strengths that carry you through to achieving your personal and relationship goals. One of your strengths may be commitment to marriage. One of your weaknesses may be managing finances together. Your commitment to each other can keep you together and give you the ability to work through the problem of finances. In fact, commitment to marriage can be a major strength because research has shown that most married couples who are committed to their marriage, yet currently struggling, will find their marriage to be happy within five years.

Wrapping It Up

This chapter was designed for you to get a better idea of where you have come from. We hope that you have learned more about where many of the relationship patterns originated that you and your spouse have. There have been many generations of people and relationships that have led up to you being you. Some have contributed tremendous gifts and strengths. Others have bequeathed you challenges and opportunities to grow.

Blaming those who have come before you will not be helpful to your present or future. However, by gaining understanding of your past and family of origin, you gain a greater freedom to choose what sort of life and marriage you want to have. Ultimately, the responsibility is yours to work on your marriage. How you and your sweetheart work through the challenges will greatly affect those around you, especially your children. They will learn from you how to be in a relationship. They will learn from you what it means to be husband and wife. "You are here." You are at the crossroads of the past and the future. What legacy do you want to leave to those who follow you?

CHAPTER 16
Managing Your Emotions

THE KEY: Being able to manage your emotions can help you work through challenges better, communicate more effectively, and increase marital intimacy.

L et's face it; we all have to deal with anger, disappointment, fear, and hurt. Those kinds of emotions tend to show up more frequently in close relationships such as family and marriages.

We hope you noticed that this chapter is on "emotional" regulation and not "how to manage your anger." Anger often gets more attention than other emotions because it is typically directed outward and can cause serious physical damage to property and to others. But anger is just one of the emotions that we need to check in order to communicate more effectively in relationships. The good news is that there is logic and a pattern that we can use for managing most emotions like anger, hurt, and fear.

Although this is somewhat stereotypical, men often feel that there is no logic involved in emotional responses. For those husbands reading this book, yes, we are saying that emotions have logic to them! Once you learn the logic of emotions, the process of managing your emotions becomes much easier. The other ingenious part of learning the logic of emotions is that you will be better able to support your spouse when he or she is experiencing strong emotions.

Emotions

Emotions can be thought of as existing at different levels; they start at a primary level and move up toward secondary levels. Just as in school, primary emotions are similar to the initial elementary grades—they are the basic emotions. However (and this is a very big however), just because primary emotions are simple and basic, they are *the* most powerful. They are the most powerful because they are the purest emotion. Secondary emotions are also powerful, but they often are a combination of primary emotions watered down by thoughts. Secondary emotions are more complex, just as high school is more complex than elementary school.

Another way to think about the difference of primary vs. secondary emotions is to think about soda. Primary emotions are like the pure syrup that soda is made with. Secondary emotions are the combination of carbonated water with the syrup. The straight syrup is very powerful and strong and would overwhelm most people if drunk alone. Then again, most people wouldn't appreciate drinking straight carbonated water either. It takes a good combination of carbonated water and syrup to have your soda just right. As with soda, people have a different preference for the "strength" of emotion that they prefer.

The main primary emotions that tend to be most relevant in marriage are love, fear, and hurt. Secondary emotions tend to be things like infatuation, anger, and frustration. For the rest of this chapter, we will focus on working with and working through hurt and fear.

Recognizing and Dealing with Emotions

So how are different emotional levels related to one another? This is where the logic of emotion comes in. Perhaps it would be helpful if we used another metaphor. Imagine you have a four- or five-year-old child—a girl who you are responsible for and who you are very fond of. Children that age live for the most part in pure, unadulterated primary emotion. They don't know how to hide very well what they are truly feeling.

You and she are cruising around the mall and she gets scared as a stranger starts to approach the two of you. The look in the child's face shows that clearly she is scared. What would you do? Most likely you would protect her or shield her in some way so as to help her not be afraid. You have several shielding or protective options at your disposal. You could try to intimidate, threaten, or flat-out physically attack the approaching stranger so that the stranger will leave. You could just pick up the child and walk away from the situation. You could chastise the child for being scared and tell her to "grow up" and that she "shouldn't be so scared all the time." Or you could try to distract the child by singing a song, acting silly, or offering her some candy.

Is any of this starting to look familiar? We hope so. The above shielding options would look very similar if the child were hurt instead of scared. The child in the above example represents your primary emotions. When we feel a form of hurt or fear, we tend to protect ourselves in a several main ways.

Six Defensive Responses

Here are the six defensive responses we typically use when trying to protect ourselves:

Response #1 : Anger

We try to push others away. We threaten, give ultimatums, try to intimidate, call names, criticize, and in some cases actually physically assault our partner.

Response #2 : Withdrawal

We try to run away. There are a lot of ways to "run away." You can physically leave the situation and go into another room in the house or go for a walk. Or you can mentally leave the situation. People can close themselves off by immersing themselves in a TV show or the newspaper, or just stop listening to what their partner is saying.

This reminds us of a story when an elderly man was approached by a young man and asked, "What is your secret to such a long and happy marriage." The wise man answered, "Well, my wife and I agreed that if we had a disagreement that I would go for a walk outside and she would knit. That way we could both calm down before we talked any further."

The young man was fascinated. "What an amazing way to deal with disagreements! This surely is a man who has more wisdom that I can learn from." So the young man asked the elderly man, "And what is your secret for such good health and apparent vitality?" The elderly man smiled and said, "A lot of fresh air and knitted sweaters to keep you warm in the evenings."

Response #3 : Self Blame

Sometimes we try to blame ourselves as a way of dealing with hurt and fear. While this doesn't seem to make much sense on the surface, it makes perfect sense in the context of relationships. If you can put yourself down before someone else can, it doesn't hurt as much if the other person does it. Then it is under your control. You have the primary say of when and where the hurt happens.

Response #4: Numbing

Another common way of dealing with primary emotions is to try to suppress or ignore them. It is in using this defense that most people fall into addictive kinds of behaviors. It doesn't matter what the addiction is. If the activity or substance—whether it is pornography, golf, shopping, drugs, or food—acts to numb your feelings, it has the possibility of turning into an addiction.

Response #5: Humor

Sometimes humor can be an adaptive response to fear and pain. Taken too far, it can become a weapon, as seen in biting sarcasm. It is also an effective way of distracting others from any primary emotion you may be feeling. Anytime we use the term "humor" in this chapter, we are referring to the biting, distracting humor that is used defensively.

Response #6: Minimization

If it isn't a big deal, then "it will go away on its own." Right? You're just "making too big a deal out of it. It's nothing to get upset about." Taking a reasonable appraisal of the situation in which you are hurting or afraid of is a good idea. Minimizing a legitimate emotional response will actually get in the way of intimacy and potentially backfire on your psychological and emotional health.

Up to this point we have been using general terms like *hurt* and *fear* for primary emotions. We would like to get a bit more specific and see if we can help you identify what types of hurt and fear you may be dealing with in your relationship.

We propose that 85 to 95 percent of your arguments with your spouse actually have a similar pattern to them. This dance is probably similar regardless of what you may argue about. The fuel for this dance comes in the form of one or two variations of hurt and fear. If you can identify what your part is in the dance, it is more likely that you will be able to control your part of your dance. It takes two to have an argument and only one to stop arguing.

Below is a list of primary emotions. Each word can represent a hurt or a fear. If you have actually experienced the feeling listed, then it is a *hurt*. If you are afraid of experiencing the feeling listed, then it is a *fear*. For example, take the word *abandoned*. If you have ever been or felt abandoned, it is a hurt. If you are afraid of being abandoned, it is a fear. In some cases, you can experience both forms of the emotion.

Take some time and read through the following list. Circle three to five words that describe feelings you have the most frequently in your disagreements or arguments with your spouse. Remember feeling afraid of the emotion itself counts as well. It would be helpful if your sweetheart did this exercise as well.

Some Common Primary Feelings

Abandoned

Disregarded

Devalued

Powerless

Unloved

Invalidated

Failure

Unappreciated

Inadequate

Lonely

Unlovable

Unworthy

Unattractive

Ugly

Now that you have circled three or more feelings, put them in order with "1" being the feeling that you experience the most. Now, next to each feeling that you selected, write down the way that you most often protect yourself from or deal with that particular emotion. Do you tend to push away, run away, or blame yourself? Maybe you try to numb the feeling (overeat, drink, get on the computer), or something else? What about minimizing, or humor as a distraction? Have your partner do this exercise as well.

The beneficial part of this exercise is that you now know how to reinterpret your own and your spouse's behavior during an argument. If they are using one of the six defensive responses (anger, withdrawal, self blame, numbing, humor, or minimizing), you now know which primary emotion they are trying to protect themselves from. Because you now are aware of this, their behavior can have a different meaning to you. Anger, withdrawal, self blame, numbing, humor, and minimization are signals that your partner is hurting or afraid. That is the logic of emotion.

When your partner is yelling, it may not be the best idea to tell your spouse, "I know you're really afraid of being inadequate right now and that is why you are yelling." At the very least you will come across as an armchair therapist. More likely, it may escalate the argument.

When your partner is showing one of the six defensive behaviors, the best thing to do is to take stock of what your internal reactions are. Do your best to keep yourself calm. Are any of your primary feelings or emotions being triggered?

The Pro-Relationship Response

The following response option simply connects your perceptions, feelings, and thoughts. You may notice that this option is not defensive. It is in fact the opposite; it is showing vulnerability. We are making the assumption that adults will tend to move toward connection and nurturing almost naturally when an individual they care about has expressed vulnerability. The pro-relationship response option follows a simple structure:

When _____ happens [identify what you heard or saw—a behavior], I feel _____ [state your feeling] because _____ [state your feared consequence or outcome].

Sometimes the primary emotion may sound overly dramatic for some situations and a less intense synonym may be more appropriate. We have included above many of the strongest primary emotions we see individuals deal with. Here are a couple of examples of using the pro-relationship response in dealing with primary emotions. It is important that you find your own ways of using this structure so that it sounds natural for you. For example:

- "When you were late and hadn't called [behaviors], I felt scared [feeling] because I was afraid that you had been in an accident [feared consequence]."
- "When you do the chore that you asked me to do [behavior], I feel upset [feeling] because I think that you don't trust me to

ever get it done [feared consequence]."

These kinds of responses open up space and the likelihood for clear communication. Using these examples gives your partner a chance to clarify their intentions or behavior and possibly apologize if needed. Other less complete, often defensive responses to primary emotions close the lines of communication by creating distance between the two of you. For instance, take the example above. If you had said, "When you were late and hadn't called I felt really scared." To which your spouse could have thought or said, "It's stupid to be scared because I am late." But when you add the consequence "because you might have been in an accident," the basis of your fear is clear and more likely to be understood and accepted. Your spouse may still think you are "silly" for thinking they were in an accident because they happen to be late. However, they now have a deeper understanding of you. The point of this exercise is to express your true feeling and gain a deeper understanding of each other, which creates intimacy.

We want to take you back to the example of the four- to five-year-old at the mall. As the "stranger" approaches, you realize that it is actually the mother of one of the child's good friends. The child you are with doesn't recognize this adult in a different setting.

At this point, the child's fear, while sincere and valid, is somewhat misplaced because this adult is actually someone she knows and trusts. You bend down and remind the child who this adult is, and she is no longer scared. She warms up to the adult and starts acting like herself again.

Again, we are a lot like that little girl. If there is a threat, it is a natural response to want to defend ourselves. But the problem is, the odds that your partner is intentionally trying to attack are slim. So many times our defensive reactions can be misplaced because we are defending when we don't need to. At times, it is difficult not to be defensive. Here are some steps you can use to increase the odds of using a pro-relationship response.

(1) Notice or "catch yourself" when you are feeling a primary emotion.

(2) Try to stop yourself before you say or do something you'll regret.

(3) Ask yourself, "What are the odds that my sweetheart would be saying or doing this to hurt me on purpose?"

(4) Look for three to four other explanations behind your partners' behavior.

(5) Decide how you would like to respond.

(6) Respond in that way.

You may have noticed that much of this chapter focuses on you rather than on your partner. That is because your emotions and reactions are 100 percent your responsibility. Your partner cannot make you feel or think anything.

Being in a relationship is like being in a game of catch that never ends. Divorce doesn't end it either. It just changes some of the rules. And even then, the rules aren't changed all that much. We are responsible for how we catch and throw the ball. There is little, if anything, you can do to make the other person throw or catch in a certain way. We have the responsibility to catch and throw the ball the best we can. We "throw the ball" when we speak and send all our verbal and nonverbal behaviors toward our sweetheart. We "catch the ball" when we attempt to interpret the message our partner is sending us.

If you throw a ball and it hits your partner square in the face, who is at fault? The answer is that you both bear some responsibility. Did the person throwing the ball throw it too hard or when they knew their partner wasn't ready or able to catch that kind of throw? Was the person catching the ball not paying attention; did they have the ability to catch that kind of throw?

Who is at fault is really a pointless question. The fact remains the same: someone has an imprint of a ball on their head and is most likely hurting. Blaming them doesn't seem appropriate ("You should have caught that, and I didn't throw it that hard!"). Taking too much of the blame doesn't seem appropriate either ("You're right, I walked right into it. I should catch it like you told me to.").

A much more appropriate conversation would look something like this:

> Thrower: "Are you okay? I am so sorry that hit you in the head! I was trying to aim for your hands."
> Catcher: "Ouch! That does hurt. Thank you for asking. I guess I was distracted when you threw it."
> Thrower: "I'll try to ask if you're ready next time."
> Catcher: "Sounds good. I'll let you know when I am ready."

When you take responsibility for your own thoughts, feelings, and actions, you gain confidence in yourself and your ability to respond to the challenges life can bring. This is claiming your personal power. It is one of the most liberating keys you can learn about. Once we realize we cannot do anything about anyone else's perception, behavior, or feelings, it can relieve us from a lot of guilt and from trying to either control or take responsibility for others when we shouldn't. What can we do? We can be respectful of others. We can make assertive requests of others. Ultimately, however, how the other person responds is completely their choice.

Taking responsibility for our own part in the relationship can be difficult at times. It may require us to admit to a weakness, or to say, "I'm sorry." No matter how hard it is, the benefit of taking ownership of your own "stuff" can far outweigh any difficulty. The payoff of owning your emotions and responses is the freedom of knowing that you have complete control of what, where, how, and when you want to respond in ways that will strengthen yourself and your relationship.

When someone we'll call Sarah was around nine years old, her parents went through a messy divorce. She didn't fully understand what was happening. All she knew was that Mom and Dad had been grumpy with each other lately. So when Mom announced one day that Dad would be moving out, Sarah naturally asked why. Her mom said that "Dad fell in love with another woman."

Now grown, Sarah is working hard on her second marriage. Her first husband, like her father, had an affair. Sarah trusts that Gabe, her second husband, is faithful, yet she has had a tendency to frequently ask where Gabe is, whom he is with, and what he is doing. It is understandable that given Sarah's history she is sensitive to being "abandoned again." It is equally understandable that Gabe at times isn't as patient as he would like to be with what he calls "her Spanish Inquisition."

Gabe arrived home a half hour late from work one evening and walked up to Sarah to give her a kiss. He was met by a cheek rather than her lips. Gabe who had had a long day at work and was already somewhat on edge snapped, "What did I do now?"

Sarah quickly responded, "You should know by now! Where were you?!"

Gabe then walked away and muttered under his breath, "First work, and now this . . ."

As Gabe was walking away, Sarah realized what had just happened again. "Gabe, wait. I'm sorry it came out that way. I was worried about you because you were late and let my mind start racing through all the possibilities. I know you. I trust you. I couldn't stand to lose you."

Gabe, now more open to hearing his wife responded, "Thank you. I'm sorry I didn't call to let you know that I was running late. I know that walking away doesn't help you either." By this time they are holding each other and Gabe says, "I love you too."

Smiling Sarah looks at Gabe and says, "Now, where is that kiss?"

In this interchange, Sarah and Gabe each did a couple of key things that turned the potential fight into an intimate moment. First, Sarah recognized that she was repeating a pattern that was getting in her way of giving and receiving love from Gabe. She then took a risk by being vulnerable to Gabe. That vulnerability was made easier as she remembered Gabe's love and concern for her. Sarah then apologized for her part in the interaction. There was no blame, no accusations. Gabe too apologized for his part in the interaction without blaming her.

The following are some things you can focus on to help you take responsibility for your own part in your marriage.

(1) Work on developing an increased awareness of the thought, feeling, or defensive behavior you want to change. In the above example, Sarah decided she did not want to do the "Spanish Inquisition" anymore. In her mind, she trusted Gabe. Her feelings (because of her experience with her parents' divorce and her first marriage) didn't always match what her mind would say. Her behavior toward Gabe—what she said and how she said it—tended to be defensive rather than using the "pro-relationship response".

(2) Pay attention to the situations that you tend to be defensive in. Remember, there are six ways in which you can be defensive. Sarah started to realize that she had very strong reactions to when Gabe was late and hadn't called to let her know when he would be home.

(3) Identify how you would like to respond to a situation. The next time Gabe came home late without calling, Sarah wanted to be able to approach him and say something like, "I've been so worried about you. Is everything okay?"

(4) Commit to how you would like to respond. Rehearse it in your mind or with a trusted friend. It is the same concept as the "Just say no" campaign that is run in elementary schools. Committing to a response before you get to a particular situation will increase the likelihood of success.

(5) Give yourself a break. Be realistic. You are not going to be perfect every time. Apologize when it is needed, and learn from the experience. Hopefully your sweetheart is also trying to work on their responses in those same situations. In the previous example, Gabe started to call when he knew he was going to be late. Each partner has a responsibility of how they "catch and throw the ball." As you improve in communicating and managing your emotions, your relationship will improve as well.

CHAPTER 17
When "No" Means "No"

THE KEY: Strong marriages are created by setting,
maintaining, and respecting boundaries which help
keep individuality and connection in balance.

Trying to define what a boundary is and is not is like trying to define who or what an "American" is. Most of us would describe an American as similar to ourselves. But is a California-American the same as a New Yorker? What about a Mid-Westerner and a person from the South? Each part of the country is different, yet we are all Americans.

Defining boundaries is similarly complex. But there are some features of boundaries that tie them all together. In other ways, there are differences between the various kinds of boundaries. One of the things that tie all boundaries together is that they help define and create individual, couple, family, community, and even country identities. Boundaries define where "you" end and "I" begin. Boundaries help define your relationship separate from the families you grew up in. In other words, boundaries start to separate "us" from "them," which is a positive thing as long as there is appreciation and respect for the other person or group. But individual boundaries will vary greatly from person to person.

All boundaries in marriage are built on the expectations, beliefs, and values you have brought into and/or created together in the marriage. Because of this relationship between beliefs and boundaries, boundaries provide the *rules* by which you live your life. When you live within your boundaries, or values, you derive satisfaction, fun, and inner peace. When these boundaries are crossed by yourself or others, you feel hurt, remorse, regret, guilt, and maybe shame.

Boundaries have three distinct dimensions:

- Levels
- Flexibility
- Openness

Levels

As mentioned before, boundaries are built on your beliefs, expectations, and values. These beliefs exist on different levels. The stronger your beliefs, the more they affect how you live and respond to your life. The following picture illustrates this idea. Most surface boundaries we have come in the form of ideas. As you move into the center, boundaries are

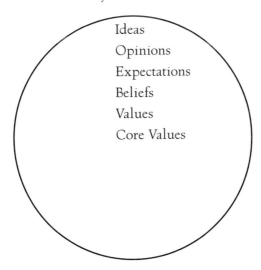

Ideas
Opinions
Expectations
Beliefs
Values
Core Values

based on beliefs, values, and core values.

Flexibility

Flexibility refers to the ability to change or adapt. How flexible a boundary is falls on a continuum from absolutely rigid to overly compromising (think children's sculpting clay). Ideally, boundaries are more flexible on the outer edges and become progressively firmer as you get closer to your core values. It is possible to have overly rigid or overly flexible (compromising) boundaries at *any* level.

You will notice that there is a gradual change in shading from the outer edge toward the middle of the next picture. This change in color represents the change from flexible boundaries on the outer part of the circle to firmer boundaries in the center.

A person with rigid boundaries comes across to other people as being a "black and white" thinker. People with rigid boundaries communicate in language that conveys a right versus wrong mentality. Probably the best way to determine if someone is setting rigid boundaries with you is when you get a feeling of being trapped, or feel there is no room for any opinions other than theirs. The best way to know when you are setting rigid boundaries is when others report feeling trapped, unaccepted, or constantly "judged."

It is perfectly appropriate and normal to have *firm* boundaries around your more central beliefs and values. Those are the guiding principles of *your* life. By having those boundaries more firm, rather than rigid, you can still have some freedom to evaluate your beliefs and values.

An overly flexible boundary is one that can change with the wind. People that are "people pleasers" tend to have overly flexible boundaries, especially around their core belief and values. They will "go with the flow" to the point that they may betray their own beliefs or values. Flexibility should not be confused with not having an opinion or belief either way on a subject. Flexibility refers to when you already have an opinion or belief and your willingness to modify or change the opinion, belief, or value. It is appropriate to have more flexible boundaries around your ideas and some opinions than values and core values. By having flexibility in these aspects, you will be more apt to learn and grow.

Openness

Openness is very closely related to flexibility. Openness refers to the

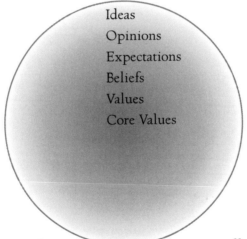

Ideas
Opinions
Expectations
Beliefs
Values
Core Values

degree which you share yourself with others as well as how much you give other people influence in your life. Typically, as a boundary becomes more flexible, it is also becoming more and more open. Rigid boundaries tend to be very closed. Because of the interrelatedness of openness and flexibility, openness ideally moves from more open at the surface toward more closed toward the core.

Most of us have run into people that are telling you their life story the first time you meet, including all the nitty-gritty details. Not only is it somewhat uncomfortable, it is inappropriate. This is an example of being too open. By being too open too quickly, you are exposing yourself to another person in a way that they could take advantage of the information you are sharing with them.

Another way of being inappropriately too open is how much influence you give another person. The most common way this happens is by asking most of your acquaintances, "What should I do about. . . ." If you frequently ask for others' opinions, how do you decide which opinion to use? In many cases, you are probably looking for someone to agree with what you have already decided. That behavior gives the appearance that anyone can tell you anything and that you will go with it.

We mentioned before that, in terms of flexibility, it was best to have *firm* boundaries around central and core values and beliefs. Firm boundaries are still somewhat open. This means that you can truly hear another person while keeping your own beliefs. You will also tend to share more central information about yourself in appropriate ways, and with appropriate relationships. As your relationship gets stronger, it is appropriate to start to open up more.

You have also met others with very closed boundaries. Often they will give very brief answers to questions or offer very little of themselves in a conversation. Another way someone may show that they are more closed is that you come away from a conversation with them saying something like, "What a delightful person." But when another friend asks you about this person you say, "They are such a delightful person . . . but I have no clue whatsoever what they like or think."

Now What?

Now that you have some concepts on the dimensions of boundaries, you can start to more easily recognize other's boundaries as well as set your own. Let's look at the next diagram. You will notice that in addition to the levels of boundaries, we have put some contexts in place. These reflect suggestions of what level of sharing might be appropriate in various contexts.

Think of someone that you would define as "professional." Why would you define them as a "professional"? These folks know that personal life will stay out of the office. They do their jobs well, regardless of what is happening in their personal life. Essentially, they have set a relatively firm, closed boundary around things not related to work when they are on the job.

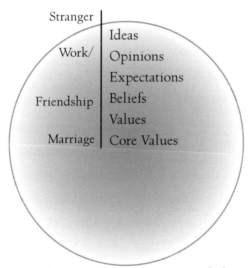

As your relationships continue to grow and deepen it becomes more appropriate for you to share your more personal beliefs, values, and even core values. The biggest difference between how you set boundaries in different contexts is how much explanation you give as to why the boundary exists. For example, a stranger comes up to you and asks you if you would like a smoke. "No, thanks" would be an appropriate response. If they pushed it further, a more firm "no" would be good.

The same situation with an acquaintance or co-worker, the response may have more detail behind the boundary (showing more openness), "No, thank you. I don't care for cigarettes." You don't necessarily have to add the "I don't care for cigarettes," if you don't want to. This does reflect more self disclosure that you may feel comfortable with in talking with a co-worker or acquaintance. If they push further as to why, you can simply repeat your statement, or say something like, "I would appreciate it if you stopped asking me."

Moving down to a friend in the same situation. (We realize that a friend most likely would not ask you to smoke with them as you have probably already set the "I don't care for cigarettes" boundary.) You could tell your friend something like, "No, thank you. I don't care for cigarettes. I watched my father die of lung cancer from smoking his pipe." You will notice an additional level of information at this level regarding some personal history.

Let's go down to the deepest level, same situation. Your spouse asks you if you want a smoke and you could say, "No thank you, I don't care for cigarettes. I watched my father die of lung cancer from smoking his pipe. I was sixteen when he passed away. He didn't get to see my prom or graduation. I am still sad when I think that he could be alive if it weren't for his smoking." This statement adds a lot more personal disclosure as to *why* the boundary exists and your personal emotional reaction to the topic. This level of communication is very appropriate in a marital setting, maybe a very close friendship as well.

Notice that the firmness of the boundary never changed in all the examples. This was a core value for the individual. The only thing that did change in each example was how open the individual was. In other words, how much space, or permission, you gave the other person to be in your world.

How to set boundaries

The first step in setting any boundary is being aware of what are your beliefs, values, and expectations. One way of identifying what your beliefs, values, or expectations are is by looking at times in the past when you may have violated your own standards or felt hurt when someone else "crossed the line" with you. Here are some other questions to think about.

- When was a time you were too rigid or flexible in the past with some of your boundaries?
- How did you use boundaries in the formation of your friendships? Were they too open? Too closed? Door mat (overly flexible, change your opinion to match those you are currently with)? Condescending (implying your boundaries were the boundaries everyone else *should* have)?
- Look at the different contexts we listed on the chart. How much of yourself do *you* think it is appropriate to disclose in those different settings?

There may be times in the past where you did set appropriate boundaries, but the other person chose to cross those boundaries anyway. Extreme but unfortunately common examples are rape, domestic and dating violence, and child abuse. Those situations say volumes about the other person. They do not say anything about your ability to set a boundary.

Once you have a rough knowledge of what your boundaries are, the next step is deciding how to set a boundary with yourself and someone else.

Setting boundaries with yourself

"Just say no." The best way to set and keep a boundary for yourself is to make the commitment to keep it. Then, identify situations in which you will need to keep that boundary for yourself. Decide now how you will handle situations like that in the future. Role play them in your mind. Do your best to follow through when the situation comes up again. You may need to decide whether or not to even put yourself in that situation again. Some of the best examples of setting boundaries for yourself come in achieving your goals, dieting, exercising, overcoming addictions, etc.

Setting boundaries with others

There are two ways to set boundaries with others: verbally or non-verbally. Verbal boundaries are sometimes the most difficult for people. A few simple rules can help.

SAY WHAT YOU MEAN

It is crucial that you match your choice of words with your intent when setting a boundary. Often people let the emotions of the moment rule their choice of words when setting a boundary. This often leads to one of two reactions. Either you give in when you don't want to, as in passionate moments, or you set an extreme boundary using words like "never" or "always" when hurt or angry. When you set a boundary with a "never," eventually you may let the other person cross your boundary down the road. This is especially true if you set the "never" boundary when you were angry or hurt. Eventually, other people will learn that your "never" does not mean never—if they nag you enough, or wait long enough, they will eventually get what they want.

When you are setting a boundary, make sure your word choice matches your values. If you say "never," you are meaning "never." If you say "not now," you are implying "maybe later." It can be difficult in the heat of the moment to choose your words carefully, but you'll be glad you did it in the long run. You won't put yourself in a situation where you feel you need to adjust an extreme boundary, or lack of one, after you have calmed down. This is why it is important to rehearse ahead of time what you want to say.

BE CONSISTENT IN YOUR BOUNDARIES

If you have chosen your words more carefully when setting a boundary, it will be easier to be consistent with that boundary. Consistency in boundaries can build esteem in yourself, and respect and trust from others. They will know where you stand on various issues. Consistency is easier to achieve as well when you have more flexible boundaries at the surface, and more firm boundaries around your core values. You won't have as many battles to fight that way, and the battles you do choose will be easier to fight. You will be able to have a clear mind as well. There isn't any, "What did I say last time?" confusion.

USE SHORT SENTENCES FOR CLEAR BOUNDARIES

Sherry was asked out on a date by her co-worker, but she did not want to date him anyway. She was dating actively at this time in her life. Try to pick out what boundary Sherry tried to set from the following:

"That is so nice of you to ask, Jerry! I've just been so busy lately with the extra projects I've had from work, I don't know when we will ever be able to make it out."

Jerry, it turns out, asked Sherry out again a month later. He knew that the extra projects that she had were done. Sherry was perplexed by this. She told her friends that she had "clearly told him that [she] wasn't interested."

Using the short sentence rule, Sherry politely told Jerry the second time he asked her out, "No thank you, Jerry. I'm not interested." It is very difficult to misinterpret this response.

BE RESPECTFUL OF YOURSELF AND THE OTHER PERSON

Sherry was respectful of herself (the second time around) by not going out on a date that she didn't want to. She was respectful of Jerry because she didn't call him names or use hurtful language. She wasn't condescending in anyway. She also did not lead him on or give him false hope. You can keep your values while respecting others.

TAKE RESPONSIBILITY (NO BLAME)

You are setting a boundary around *your* values, not anyone else's. Therefore, make your language reflect that fact. Traditional communication training programs call them "I messages." Sherry's second attempt at telling Jerry she didn't want to date him was a good example of taking responsibility. She said, "I'm not interested."

BE POSITIVE

Other people are more likely to hear a boundary that has a request for action rather than inaction. For example, "I don't appreciate being called names. I would love to talk with you if you gave me a specific complaint or example." Requests for action work best if the other person can't do the action you are requesting and the thing you don't like at the same time. Let's say that your sweetheart has an annoying habit. This is a prime situation in which you can make a positive request. "I love it when you _____." An example from a wife might be, "I love it when you kiss me with a cleanly shaved face." Non-verbal boundaries come in the form of body language. "Talk to the hand" comes to mind as a good example. Some non-verbal boundaries that we would NOT recommend include turning on the TV as the other person is talking, burying your head in a book, newspaper, or computer. Each sends a clear message that you think the other person and what they are saying is not worth your time. We DO recommend sitting or standing up straight with good posture. This helps send a message of, "I'm serious." Firm voice tone and eye contact will also help communicate importance behind your message.

Respecting other's boundaries

Now that you know how to set a boundary, the trick is recognizing when others are setting boundaries as well. The problem is that those around you are not reading this book. They may be saying "never" and not mean it, giving long confusing reasons as to why they wont agree to your request, or may be flat-out rude.

Ask for clarification

You as the listener have the job of asking for clarification to find out what the boundary they are trying to set is. It is best not to assume what you *think* they mean. "Never" may indeed mean never. You will not know for sure unless you ask for clarification. If they are hurt, or very angry, then it might not be the time to ask for clarification of the boundary they are trying to set. You might get a "Did you not hear me? I said . . ." response.

Wait until things have cooled down and approach the other person and ask for clarification. It would be best to start off by asking the other person "if now would be a good time to talk about the argument" you had. If now is not a good time, ask them when would be a good time. It may even be helpful to apologize for your part of the negative interaction before asking for clarification because by asking about the boundary, you are in fact bringing up the topic again. Once you have done that, you can ask for clarification. "Could you please tell me what else you were thinking about when you said you never wanted to discuss finances ever again?"

WARNING! If you ask such a question, you are opening yourself up for feedback on your behavior as well. Be prepared for it. Getting defensive will only bring you back to where you started. Try to put yourself in their shoes as you listen. If it would be helpful, pretend that they are a friend telling you about their spouse.

KNOW THEIR LINGO

The first year of marriage for a couple we will call Jane and Michael, was one full of "discussions" that lasted a couple of hours. Toward the end of the discussion, they found that they were actually on the same page most of the time. It was frustrating to spend all that time arguing a point, or boundary, to find out that they actually agreed. In the process of this, they learned each other's lingo. In essence, they created a translation guide for each other. By asking for clarification and getting to know your sweetheart's core values, beliefs, and expectations, you will begin to have a boundary translation guide. It needs to be pointed out though, that the translation guide may only be good for a year or two before it needs to be updated. When in doubt, get an update.

RESPECT

If your partner has set a firm boundary, you need to respect it even if you don't agree with it. You have a right to express your view, and you probably already have, but after you have expressed your view, your job as husband and wife is to love, accept, and respect each other anyway. Don't forget your differences as well as you similarities are what brought you together in the first place.

Wrapping it up

Getting to know one another's boundaries can be a painful yet productive process for all involved. It is like those first few slow dances you had together. You will inadvertently step on each other's toes. After a while of adjusting to each other, you will move together beautifully. Boundaries will help you each keep your individuality while at the same time appreciating, respecting, and loving each other and your relationship.

CHAPTER 18
Grieving

THE KEY: In a great marriage, husbands and wives support each other in the grieving process.

It may seem odd to some of you that grief is included as an essential key to a successful marriage. Spouses, individually and together, will experience events and losses in their lives for which grieving is appropriate and necessary. While painful to go through, grieving is one of the most liberating things individuals and couples can do together. Grieving helps people work through loss while giving a new and wonderful perspective on life. It is one of life's paradoxes that by moving through the grief process you will be able to find greater peace and happiness.

Finding Your Own Grieving Process

Grief traditionally has been described as a step-by-step process. As you complete each step you transition to the next. First you go through shock, then denial, anger, sadness, and finally acceptance. All done. Right? Not necessarily. While most people do experience these emotions, they don't always follow a step-by-step pattern. After reading about a step-like grieving process, some people may feel they have reached acceptance and therefore are "done" grieving a particular loss. If they ever start to feel sad again, or even angry, they start to beat themselves up because they've "been through that" already. They question whether or not they have grieved at all.

That isn't helpful for anyone, especially when you are trying to deal with and move through a loss. In fact, most people jump around among the different "steps" as they go through the grieving process. Some people may feel acceptance of the loss initially, then shock, denial, sadness, or anger, and then back to acceptance. Many of you might experience several emotions simultaneously. Each time you go through these various emotions, you may feel them for a different length of time, different intensity, or different frequency. It is normal to go through all the emotions of grief several times. Each time you go through an emotion of the grieving "process," hopefully it becomes less intense—not lasting as long or coming as frequently.

Take a few moments and think about a loss you have experienced. It could have been the death of a loved one, the loss of a pet, or a breakup. Below is a list of typical emotions people experience as they grieve. First, think about and recall your loss. Then put the emotions you experienced in chronological order. For example, put a number 1 next to what you were initially feeling. Put a number 2 by the second emotion you experienced, and so on.

- Shock
- Denial
- Anger
- Sadness
- Acceptance

Pick and choose another experience of loss and do the same thing.

Were your answers to the two grieving experiences similar? If so, you have found a pattern to your unique grieving process. If not, don't worry—your grieving process simply may change depending on the kind of loss and stage of life you are in. Have your spouse do the same exercise. What is his or her process? How does it differ from yours? If you and your spouse have different processes, how does this knowledge help you better understand past grieving experiences you have had together? Before we talk more about the grieving process, it is helpful to determine the kind of loss you are grieving.

Tangible versus Intangible Loss

What do people grieve about? The short answer to that question is "You can grieve any loss that you experience." The next question then becomes "What is a 'loss'?" Simply put, loss represents the discrepancy between what "is" in the here and now, and what the present "should" or "could" be like. Loss can be expected, such as the last child leaving home or the death of an elderly parent. Loss can also be unexpected as happens with layoffs, accidents, or a spouse's habit you had no idea about before you were married. Some loss is tangible, or visible to you and others. A tangible loss could be any of the following:

- death of a loved one
- stolen property
- house fire
- death of a pet
- physical injury (e.g., paralysis)
- bankruptcy
- divorce

Tangible losses are difficult, and intangible losses can be every bit as difficult. However, intangible losses are often more difficult to grieve because not everyone can see the loss. It is easy for others to see when a loved one dies, or when a catastrophe hits home. With intangible loss, your life may look all right from the outside and yet you still have a need to grieve. Intangible loss is when you have a dream, hope, or expectation that has not been (or seems not to be able to be) fulfilled. Below is a brief list of intangible losses:

- rejection from the college of your choice
- not hired for your dream job
- rejection of a marriage proposal
- emotional divorce
- mismatch of the way things are and the way you think they should be
- a lost opportunity
- infertility

With intangible losses, well-meaning family and friends often encourage you to "move on," or "get over it." They say things like "It could be worse," "Let it go," and the ever popular, "Life isn't fair." These comments only tend to make you feel worse.

Most loss actually includes some combination of physical, tangible loss and internal, intangible loss. When we marry, whether we can talk about it or not, we create a vision of "happily ever after" in our minds. We have a sense of what we think it will be like to be with this person for the rest of our lives. Some women see the kids, homes, and a pair of rocking chairs on the front porch of their future home in the country. Even the guys have a "happily ever after" in their minds. It may be that they see their wives with them through their accomplishments and activities. The "happily ever after" is the intangible piece of marriage that is grieved when you realized that the marriage is not headed on that track, or when a spouse is lost to death or divorce.

Now What? Getting Started on the Path

No matter the type of loss, grieving takes time and likely a similar path. Perhaps you have already identified your unique path through the emotions of grief. Below is a list of steps that can help you through your grieving process. We will not tell you when you should or shouldn't be "done" grieving a particular loss. The "final" step does not mean you are done. These steps are to help you to get started grieving. You decide when you are done.

STEP 1: RECOGNIZE THE NEED TO GRIEVE

The first step to grieving is recognizing that you need to grieve. Often symptoms of mild to moderate depression can be confused with emotions and behaviors related to grief. For example, crying easily, feeling agitated or irritable, not wanting to do things you used to, sleep problems, changes in diet, and so on are all symptoms of depression as well as bereavement. The tip-off that you may be experiencing the need to grieve rather than experience depression is that you can identify a reason for the symptoms.

By "reason," we mean that when you talk about your symptoms, there is a common thread that ties them together. For example, you liked to golf with your dad and since he passed away you really haven't felt the urge to golf. Or, you tend to cry when you hear or see something that reminds you of happy memories growing up (with dad). If you find yourself having many of the symptoms we listed above, talk with a mental health professional. They will be able to help you determine if you are experiencing clinical depression, or bereavement.

A woman we'll call Joanne went into a therapist's office complaining that she was having problems with sleep, readily cried, and tended to be a bit more "on edge" lately. She thought that she might be depressed, but wasn't sure. Joanne wasn't suicidal, she functioned very well in her professional life, and her marriage had the normal ups and downs. She just "hadn't been herself lately." As Joanne was talking with her therapist, she disclosed that she lost her mother to cancer about a year previously. She had recently had a major change in her career, which she wasn't as confident in, and her youngest child just started her senior year of high school.

After the loss of her mother, whom she was very close to, Joanne "pulled herself up by the boot straps," and went on with life. Any thought of her mother wasn't "indulged," and was considered "silly." Her daughter, whom she was also very close to, was making plans for college and probably would be moving out of state the following year. Again, Joanne dismissed any thoughts about this other than, "That's what kids do; they grow up and become responsible adults." As Joanne talked about these two important women in her life, she started crying again. "See, this is what happens all the time," she said. Joanne had not discussed these things with her husband or daughter.

It was suggested that Joanne needed to grieve not only the loss of her mother, but she also might want to consider that she needed to grieve the loss of being a mother in the same way to her daughter. She was able to recognize that her "symptoms" were not depression at all; she had needed to grieve. And she learned that it would be helpful to include her husband in that process.

Step 2: Emotional surfing

After Joanne recognized that she needed to grieve, she learned about emotional surfing. Emotional surfing is the fancy way of giving yourself permission to experience your emotions. When you start to feel sad, let yourself feel sad. Sure, the emotions may be more intense at first. They won't hang around for as long though. If it is not a good time to allow yourself to surf the emotional wave, such as at work, give yourself permission to do it later in the day.

For many people, ignoring the emotions of grief only makes them stronger and more difficult to control. It is like trying to stop a wave on the ocean. If the wave is big enough, it will take you with it and tumble you around on the bottom. By going with the wave, you can maintain some control of yourself while you are on the wave and then somewhat smoothly get off the wave. Use this emotional energy to your advantage.

Another way to think about this concept is to imagine you are a martial arts expert. What do you do when another person throws a punch at you? Do you try to catch the punch in mid air to stop it? Hopefully not. You are more likely to break your hand that way. Or the momentum of their punch will force you to be hit with your own hand. Trying to just "stop" emotions is the same way. You'll just end up getting hurt in the process. It is better to validate the emotions in yourself. This is akin to deflecting the punch and using the other person's energy against him. Joanne did this by saying things like, "I'm really going to miss being a full-time mom" and "I'm sure my mother would have loved . . ." Even by making a statement such as, "I feel sad right now" can take much of the sting away from the emotions as you go with the flow of the emotion.

Step 3: Use the buddy system

We are social beings. Having people to support you such as your spouse, family, and friends goes a long way in moving through the grief process. You strengthen relationships by mourning with those who are mourning.

A hiccup when you are grieving and looking for emotional support is that other people will not know what you need from them. So, tell them up front what you need. You could go to your sweetheart and say something like, "I need you to listen right now. I want to talk about . . ." Or maybe when you need some space, "I appreciate you wanting to be here right now for me; I just need an hour or so alone."

Other hiccups when using a support system during grief is assuming that the other people will "get it," or they will make it "go away." Most people can have some empathy for you, but rarely will someone be able to fully "get it" or understand how you are feeling. You are the expert on you, and you will be the best person to identify and take care of your emotions. The same is true about others being able to make it "go away," or make it "all better." They can be there to support you, but they can't fix it for you. Only you and time can do that.

STEP 4: TRACK IT

Many times in life, we are growing and healing and we don't even know it. On the next page is a chart you can use through the grief process. You will notice that each column is one of the grief emotions. Within each emotion is a "D," "I," and "F." The "D" stands for *duration*. When you are grieving, write down a number on the chart indicating how long, on average, you feel that particular emotion when it comes. The number may reflect seconds, minutes, hours, days, or weeks. The "I" stands for *intensity*. This is for you to record the intensity of the particular emotion you are recording. Usually intensity is on a scale from 1–10 with 10 being the most intense and 1 being mild. The "F" stands for *frequency*. You simply record how many times you felt that particular emotion in the time period listed.

Let's say you felt in shock about 2 hours when your loss hit you in the first week. When it hit you, the intensity was an average of an 8. Finally, let's say that you felt shocked four times that week. Your chart would look like:

Shock			
	D	I	F
1st Week	2hrs.	8	4

Record each emotion every week if you would like. Our suggestions for emotions to track include shock, denial, anger, saddness, and acceptance. The chart separates out the time more as you get farther from when you started to record your feelings. When you get to the line for "8 weeks," simply record what you have been feeling for that previous month. As you look down each column, hopefully you see that the duration, intensity, and frequency of each emotion has decreased over time.

Grieving Can Liberate You

We've mentioned several times in this chapter that grief can liberate you. Now it is time to show you how that works.

There is no such thing as a perfect relationship, or perfect partner. Some of you may be agreeing more with that last statement than others. As you have gone through other chapters of this book, your expectations for what a "good" husband, wife, and marriage should be clearer to you by now.

What may also be clear is how you, your spouse, and your marriage do not completely or always match your expectations. You may be well on your way to recognizing that you, or your spouse, may not be able to meet those expectations in certain areas exactly as you have dreamed about them.

Notice that we said exactly. You can grieve the loss of that specific dream. Once you have done that, you are now open to what your relationship can become in those areas. When you shift from what "should be" to what "can be," your whole attitude and outlook changes. You move from sadness and regret to hope. You start looking for signs of movement toward what "can be" rather than finding evidence that "it will never be." This is not the same thing as *lowering* your expectations. It is *changing* your expectations.

Let's look at what your relationship was like, and what state of mind you were in, when you made those "happily ever afters" to begin with. You probably created those dreams and expectations while you were dating and during your engagement. The "happily ever afters" were created at a time when you each were on your best behavior at least 95 percent of the time. For every one or two little negative interaction, there were ten, twenty, or thirty positives to overshadow them. Would you say that this was a good time to make an accurate assessment of what was possible for your marriage? It may be accurate if you both are still on your best behavior 95 percent of the time.

Please understand, it is good to have dreams and expectations for yourself, your partner, and your marriage. All that we are saying is, now that you have had time to adjust more to your sweetheart (warts and all), it is a good time to revisit your "happily ever after."

If you don't want to change anything, try setting time by which you would like those dreams fulfilled. One mistake many people make is they assume that their marriage has to match their "happily every after" immediately. That impatience is not fair to either partner. First of all, you may be acting according to your expectations in your dreams, but are you acting how your sweetheart would like you to act in their dreams? Please remember that when you look at couples that are currently happy after twenty, thirty, or forty years of marriage, that it has taken them twenty, thirty, or forty years to get to that place. Give yourself and your partner a little time too.

The best, and frequently most realized, "happily ever afters" are coauthored. They take the best from each of your dreams and combine them. So, in many ways, the best idea is for each of you to grieve your individual "happily ever after" and then find your common dream, *our* marital "happily ever after."

Grief is a critical part of life. In some ways the grieving process is a skill. And remember that skills can be enhanced. By grieving any loss, you respect the value of the loss. You create an opportunity to be supported by, or supportive to, your sweetheart. Ultimately, you get to find hope in what is possible in your life, rather than to keep finding the holes. With that, we wish you the most meaningful of life through grief and wish you to find that hope and peace that is in store for all of us.

CHAPTER 19
The Power of Forgiveness

THE KEY: Forgiving others and yourself is crucial to building and reinforcing a strong marriage.

When couples are trying to work through a difficult or painful experience, they often say something like, "We just wish we could have our old relationship back." Why would they want that? It doesn't make sense. Didn't the old relationship set the context for the painful experience they are trying to work through? It makes much more sense to focus on the strengths of the relationship now and what the marriage can become from here on. With forgiveness, the relationship can become much better than it ever has been.

For many years, the topic of forgiveness has stayed in the realm of religion and spirituality. Increasingly, however, professional therapists, family therapists, and social scientists have started taking a great interest in forgiveness. The more they study forgiveness, the more they realize its importance.

The major benefit of forgiveness—specifically, forgiving—is the psychological and emotional freedom it brings. In addition, individuals who are forgiving also tend to have better physical health. Forgiveness is ultimately for you, not for anyone else.

Conversely, an unforgiving attitude leaves little emotional and psychological energy for other parts of life. Being caught up in the past drains a person's energy. People cannot focus on both the past and the here-and-now.

Lack of forgiveness is often accompanied by feelings of anger, sadness, and bitterness, which can be stressful. Prolonged stress is one of the body's worst enemies (see chapter 22). When you've become convinced that forgiving is a good thing, the next challenge lies in defining what forgiveness is and how to do it.

Forgiveness is *not*:

- Forgetting what happened.
- Pretending the natural consequences of actions don't exist.
- Automatically trusting.
- Vulnerability or weakness.
- Letting the other person off the hook.
- Condoning hurtful behavior.

For the offended person, forgiveness *is*:

- Understanding of self and others.
- Accepting of self, others, and situations.
- An internal journey.
- An opportunity for possible reconciliation.
- A relational building block.
- A chance to create personal boundaries and protect oneself.
- Strength.
- Good for mental, emotional, physical, spiritual, and (usually) relational health.

• Required for internal peace.

Offenses are an interesting thing. In chapter 4, Seeing Through Rose-Colored Glasses, you read about the difference between an event and the meaning of the event. This principle is also crucial in the process of forgiveness. If you perceive an event as an attack on your character or physical or emotional safety, the process of forgiveness will be more difficult. Sometimes one person intends to hurt the other, but this is rare in a great marriage. More often than not, the offending spouse is not aware of the hurt to his or her sweetheart. Generally, neither partner intends to hurt the other. So why do many of us assume that offenses are intentional? The ability to recognize your own contribution to offenses as well as your partner's will help you reconcile differences and strengthen your marriage.

The Forgiveness Courtroom

One way of thinking about the process of forgiveness is to imagine yourself in a courtroom setting. There are six main roles in a courtroom:

- Judge
- Jury
- Prosecuting attorney
- Defense attorney
- Executioner
- Witness

Five of these roles hamper forgiveness. However, the sixth role, witness, puts you in a good place in terms of forgiveness. Below is a description of each role, along with examples to help you determine which role you may be playing in your marriage.

JUDGE

The judge's role is to assign responsibility, blame, or guilt, and to determine punishment. In jury trials, the judge guides the course of the arguments and gives instructions to the jury concerning evidence they can and cannot use for a verdict.

In relationships, people become judges when they decide who is at fault and what the punishment should be. Judging is appropriate in a parenting situation. However, your spouse is not your child, but your equal.

Acting as a judge in your marriage assumes you are on a higher level than your spouse. You assume power, and by so doing, you can "overrule" any idea, thought, feeling, or opinion of your sweetheart. This assumption of power is damaging and can get in the way of forgiveness. However, using your judgment to determine whether a situation is emotionally and physically safe is appropriate. Using your judgment is the basis to make decisions for you own responses and behavior, not someone else's. Being a judge puts the focus away from you and onto on another's responses and behaviors.

A good example of being a judge versus using your judgment can be found in the story of Julie and James. James consistently pushed and eventually coerced Julie to engage in actions that were contrary to her moral code, even to the point of acting against her deepest values. When she attempted to set a boundary and follow her value system, she felt guilty, so she would give in to James' repeated requests. The pattern escalated until they were on the verge of divorce.

Julie assumed the judge role in this situation by consistently blaming James; she even went as far as diagnosing his mental condition. She then shared this diagnosis with everyone close to her in her life.

He "wasn't worthy" of her time, and she felt completely justified in pursuing divorce.

But with counseling Julie learned to use her judgment in a positive way to determine that she wanted to follow her value system, of which being committed to marriage was a value of hers. She realized that staying married to James would be very difficult in the short run, but it was what she wanted in the long term. They had tried several avenues to reconcile and show respect to each other's belief and value systems. Julie gave herself permission to maintain boundaries without feeling guilty. She stopped diagnosing her husband's "problems" and began to see him as a mere human with shortcomings, just like herself. James also learned to see his role in the interaction and they worked in forgiving one another without judging each other any more.

JURY

Ideally, a jury is a group of non-biased peers who assign guilt and responsibility. However, in reality, attorneys do everything they can to select a jury that will side with them. We all do this; when we're hurt, we naturally go to friends and family members for support. Rarely do friends and families "rule" on the side of the other person; instead, they sympathize with us and give us the validation we are looking for.

Both James and Julie attempted to collect a jury. Each appealed to friends, family, and therapists for support. Each story was equally believable. After they reconciled, they had to deal with one of the pitfalls of collecting a jury: they moved through the hurt more quickly than their respective juries did. In other words, you may have forgiven your partner, but the next time you see your friend (a juror), she'll probably bring up how wrong your spouse was. You may have done such a good job presenting your case that when you reconcile, your jury will believe that you have been "suckered" back into the relationship. A lesson here is that it is rarely a good idea to seek sympathy or "confide" in friends or family when you are in conflict with your spouse.

DEFENSE AND PROSECUTING ATTORNEYS

In your marriage, you may be both the defense and prosecuting attorney at the same time. You will try to prove your innocence (defense) while simultaneously trying to prove your partner's guilt (prosecution).

Defense attorneys often help their clients deny all responsibility or accountability. They blame other people, the client's background, or an unfortunate situation in their attempt to prove innocence. Blaming is a huge obstacle to reconciliation because true forgiveness requires each spouse to take ownership for his or her part in the relationship, in addition to forgiving the other person.

To present the strongest case possible, prosecuting attorneys look for the tiniest shreds of evidence. They also try to use the defense's evidence to their own advantage. A prosecutor presents evidence showing that their own client is an innocent victim who has absolutely no responsibility for the situation. While this may be true in crime cases, in marriage there are two people with responsibility for the relationship.

Both James and Julie told about being wronged, misunderstood, or victimized. Each claimed their spouse rarely did anything worth appreciating. Any kindness or goodness the spouse showed was "a cover" and not the spouse's true self.

One of the problems of becoming a defense or prosecuting attorney in a relationship is putting others in a position to take sides. Some will be comfortable siding with you. But people who feel loyalty to both of you are placed in a no-win situation. No matter which side they choose, they lose a relationship with the other side. Children of spouses who play these roles can be especially damaged; the children love unconditionally and want to make both parents happy. Even adult children struggle with being placed in the position of jury to their parents' roles of prosecution or defense.

Executioner

In many ways, the executioner's job is the simplest. He carries out the punishment decided on by the judge and jury. He is not held responsible for his actions, as he is merely giving the convicted criminal "what he deserves."

In a marriage, this role can be very time-consuming and require an enormous amount of psychological and emotional energy. Executioners may disguise themselves as crusaders, or they may instigate a vendetta. As an executioner, your life will be consumed with making sure "no one else will be hurt" like you were. If your other relationships are paying the price of your crusade, it may be time to reconsider the value of your quest. You may unintentionally push those close to you toward the person you are crusading against. James became an executioner when Julie would make a reasonable request or statement, and then James would ignore, withdraw, or even attack Julie. Julie did the same with James.

Witness

The witness's role is "to tell the whole truth, and nothing but the truth." Witnesses are allowed to explain their emotional reactions to a situation. Their job is to tell their story, to tell what the experience was like for them.

Forgiveness requires giving up the role of judge, jury, prosecution or defense, and executioner to a higher power. To forgive, you must assume the role of the witness.

To be a witness requires that you must own your experience—your thoughts, feelings, and actions. The other roles in the courtroom are turned over to your higher power who you must trust to execute wise, fair, and efficient judgment and punishment. To give up the unhealthy roles and achieve the role of witness, some people use ideas based in religious philosophy, such as karma, prayer, meditation, and rituals.

Healthy Forgiveness

At polar ends of the forgiveness continuum are acceptance and complete reconciliation/restoration of the relationship. Restoration is this context refers to repairing the relationship, in most cases with a stronger and deeper bond than before. Becoming a "witness" is a critical step on each end.

Acceptance

This end of the forgiveness continuum is an internal process. That is, no one else needs to be involved for you to achieve the emotional and psychological freedom that it offers. This level of forgiveness is particularly important when reconciliation is not possible, as in the death or severe impairment of the other person. It is also appropriate when continuation of the relationship would be physically or emotionally dangerous.

Following are a few steps that will help you through the process of acceptance:

1. Pick a specific event for which you want to forgive yourself or someone else.
2. Describe the event.
    (a) Try to imagine that you are directing actors to reenact the event.
    (b) Include what happened, who said what, and who did what.
3. Describe your experience.
    (a) What were your thoughts when _____ happened?
    (b) What were your feelings when _____ happened?
    (c) How did you react?
    (d) What was your part in the experience or event?
4. Try to describe the other person's experience.
    (a) What were the other person's thoughts when _____ _____ happened?
    (b) What were his or her feelings when _____ happened?
    (c) How did the other person react?
    (d) What was his or her part in the experience or event?
5. Give yourself permission to "have" your thoughts and feelings.
    (a) Write in a journal.
    (b) Tell a trusted friend, ecclesiastical leader, or professional counselor.
    (c) Imagine how you would respond to a friend who told you a similar experience.
6. Be a witness, not executioner, judge, or jury. Trust that a higher power will execute fair judgment.

Reconciliation and Restoration

The other end of the healthy forgiveness continuum—reconciliation—often helps the relationship become stronger and more resilient. In this sense, *restoration* refers to the continuation of the relationship, but not necessarily a return to "the way it was." A "return to normal" refers to the past relationship. But reconciliation can move a relationship toward the future and to a higher level.

The first three steps of reconciliation are identical to those of acceptance. The difference is that you disclose this information to the person who hurt you. You can skip step four because you will get the chance to hear about your partner's thoughts and feelings, so you don't need to guess. The other person may not be aware of your hurt feelings. When you disclose them, you give your spouse a chance to apologize and make things right if necessary.

A specific emotional environment helps these kinds of discussions to work well. Both individuals must value the relationship more than their own egos. This is easier said than done. If pride creeps in, defensiveness and blame will come with it. If defensiveness and blame surface, reconciliation will be short-circuited.

When you finish telling the other person about your feelings regarding a hurtful event, you must listen to his or her reactions and feeling about the same event. You are now in the position to hear how your actions may have contributed to the situation. It is crucial that you love your sweetheart during this exchange. There is no room for martyrs in reconciliation. You had a part in the event. Making yourself vulnerable may be scary, but it can be very liberating, both for the individuals and for the relationship. Through listening to some feedback from the other person, you have the opportunity to grow personally and in your relationship.

After you each express your side of the event using the acceptance steps, you then move on to reconciliation. Follow these steps:

1. *Apologize for your part in the event.* No one is perfect. We all make mistakes in relationships, especially when we are reacting to what we perceive to be a threat or intentional harm. Individuals tend to attack back, withdraw from the relationship, avoid the topic or person, try to escape through things like alcohol or drugs, use humor inappropriately to distract from the importance of the situation, or minimize. Any of these behaviors can be apologized for.

2. *If appropriate, make plans for restitution.* Restitution can be as simple as replacing a broken object or as complex as trying to restore trust. Restoration of trust can be a big challenge. There are two parts to restoring trust. The biggest challenge facing the offending spouse is patience. She needs to focus on making changes for personal reasons as well as trying to regain her spouse's trust. This is especially important after abuse or an affair. The more the offending spouse asks, "When are you going to just trust me?" the less the likelihood that trust will be restored.

The hurt spouse faces the challenge of determining when he can trust again. He may experience a strong temptation to become a judge by thinking things like, "She doesn't deserve my trust." A more helpful, and probably more truthful, thought is, "I'm not ready to trust yet." Try to think of trust in terms of levels rather than all-or-nothing, like using a dimmer knob rather than a light switch. You can slowly turn up the dimmer (trust level), rather than settling for total light or darkness (complete trust or distrust).

3. *Commit to continued individual and relational growth.* This is the

rewarding part of reconciliation. At this stage, couples are ready to "move on." Some couples may choose to take part in a "forgiveness ritual" to symbolize they are closing the door on one stage of their relationship and moving on to a new stage.

Forgiveness Rituals

A very helpful tool in the step of committing to continued growth is the use of forgiveness rituals, or some kind of ceremony with meaningful symbols. Symbols can be anything, but make sure the symbol(s) you choose in your forgiveness ritual are meaningful to both parties involved. The following is a list of helpful rituals. It is by no means exhaustive.

Bury the Hatchet

Find a symbol that represents your previous negative interactions and literally bury it. Take a toy hatchet or make one out of cardboard and go out in the garden, dig a hole, and bury it. This ritual works best if you have a new symbol of your current, positive, interaction patterns to replace the buried hatchet.

Renewal of Marital Vows

Some couple's enjoy the ritual of renewing their marital vows. This can be a great way to start a "new" relationship, especially if you write new vows. The process of writing joint vows or editing each other's vows can be fun and useful, too. Maybe you know more now!

Burning

Find a symbol (sometimes a written document) that represents the past hurtful events and burn it. Or write down the things you want to let go of on a paper and burn that. As a part of the ceremony, include and celebrate something to show commitment to the type of "new" relationship that you both want After Alice and Al burned the paid student loan bills, they put the "paid in full" certificate in their scrapbook. This can provide a reference point for your relationship and evidence of a new beginning.

Balloon Release

Write down painful feelings or memories. Consider using code words or pictures to represent those memories or feelings, rather than actual statements that could be read and understood by someone else. (Don't include names or identifying information, as the balloons will eventually pop or come down somewhere. Also, be judicious in your use of balloons.) Attach them to a balloon, and "let them go" up, up and away, signifying your release from those feelings or memories.

Wrapping It Up

The forgiveness process that has been discussed seems very formal. The more painful the hurt or event, the more a formal process can be incredibly helpful. The structure of a formal process gives security and safety as you work through the forgiveness process. Minor miscommunications or misunderstandings may not require this formal process. Simply discussing with each other your thoughts, feelings, and reactions can help clarify perceptions and smooth things out. Once you have a clearer understanding of where you each stand, the hurt feelings often disappear, because small forgiveness has occurred.

Forgiveness can help you gain insight into both your own psyche and your sweetheart's perceptions. As your understanding of each other increases, you'll be less likely to take offense at certain behaviors.

The less you become offended, the more happiness and freedom you will experience in your relationship.

Chapter 20
Laughter is the Best Medicine

THE KEY: In successful marriages husbands and wives draw on appropriate humor and laugh together.

E very day things happen around us, and to us, that are funny. Or at least they can be seen as funny. Humor is a multi-billion dollar industry (including sitcoms, comedy clubs, movies, and so on). It doesn't matter what strikes your funny bone—most people love to laugh. Have you ever thought of why we laugh? What purpose does it have? Why do we value it so much? And what does it have to do with marriage? As you read on, you will see that humor and laughter play a critical role in your marital and physical health.

In this chapter, we use both the words *humor* and *laughter*. We use these terms interchangeably. Some people don't laugh out loud but still find things very humorous or amusing. These individuals will get the same benefits as those of you that laugh out loud.

Individual Effects of Laughter

Noted author and editor Norman Cousins believed in the healing powers of laughter. In the face of a severe illness, he made it a point to "belly laugh" every day in addition to his medical regime. He completely recovered from the illness and attributed his recovery partly to laughter. Laughter can be a powerful healer.

Research and science has shown that there is something to Cousins' approach. The immune system increases its functioning when a person's mood is elevated (for example, through laughing) . When the immune system functions better, you will tend to heal more quickly and get sick less often. Laughter can also lower your blood pressure.

Humor is inexpensive and readily available. It has almost no side effects and can be a way of temporarily and naturally treating stress, anxiety, and depression. While not necessarily *addictive*, it has been found that laughter is *contagious*. However, humor at your partner's expense will have some unwanted side effects. Other than that, the biggest side effects of using humor to combat stress, anxiety, or depression may be a side ache! Laughter can be really good exercise to boot.

Laughter is especially helpful in combating stressful situations and events if you can find a way to make those events humorous or find humor in them. Humor has a great way of putting things in perspective, much in the same way as stress has a way of blowing things out of perspective.

Relational Effects of Humor

A genuine smile is often all it takes to draw another person toward you. Humor and laughter have the same effect. Laughter will tend to bind you and your spouse together. If you are laughing about a stressful situation, your sweetheart may start to laugh as well. Then you both get to benefit from the individual effects of laughter and are able to strengthen your relationship as well.

Humans are hardwired to connect—to be open and friendly, especially with those people we care about or who are close to us personally and emotionally. Laughter is very powerful in generating curiosity in others, which in turn draws them toward you. For example, if someone in your office is laughing and you ask, "What's so funny?" how would you respond if they say, "It's nothing really." Typically with that response you will persist and ask again. Or, have you ever been walking down the hall or street and heard a group of people laughing? What was your response? If you are like most people you slowed down to see (and hear) what was going on. At the very least you would have wondered what they were laughing about. There is a natural tendency to want to be in on the joke, to be included in the group, to enjoy the laugh.

Adults don't laugh often throughout the day. It has been observed that adults laugh about 15 times a day while children laugh some 400 times a day! Because we were all children once, that is a significant loss for us as adults. How about you and your spouse? Do you laugh as much as your children or as much as you used to when you were a child? Perhaps adults are too serious? When couples and individuals are struggling in life, the number of times they laugh drops even more. Stress and all its nasty side effects will start to take over. Yet, humor and laughter are powerful antidotes to stress. Humor and laughter can bring the two of you together in both stressful and nonstressful times. As mentioned before, humor can put problems into perspective so they don't seem so big.

Try laughing together if you want to "reignite the spark" or "warm things up" in your marriage. Laughter and the process of having a good laugh will go a long way towards the goal of coming together. Many times when couples are trying to "heat things up" they are trying to gain a greater sense of excitement and connection, which typically plays out in the sexual arena. Laughing together can also create an environment of greater excitement and connection that lingers for a longer time than some new technique in the bedroom. The lingering happens because you are connected at an emotional and psychological level rather than just physically.

Do adults naturally grow out of mirth and jollity? Humor and laughter will come somewhat naturally, especially if you are able to remember how to play. Children are good at play and perhaps that is why they laugh so much more than adults. The ability to play is one of the adult's most neglected and forgotten talents. And yet, we all had the talent of playfulness at one time. When we were kids almost any activity could be—and often was—made into play or an amusement. There was no schedule to the play. Now as adults, everything is a task, chore, or duty. Take for example, washing the car. Watch two adults wash the car, and then watch a couple of teens wash the car. Then if you are brave enough to be outside at the time, watch a couple of five-to eight-year-olds wash the car. What is the difference?

The adults are more concerned about "getting the job done, and done right." They will also be the driest when the job is done. As the groups get younger, you will observe that they will be progressively wetter. Yet the car will be washed nonetheless. The younger groups will also have had more fun, more laughter, more connectedness, and *less stress.* Much of the potential for humor and fun is lost once something becomes a chore or duty.

To enhance your ability to approach things more playfully, discuss the following with your spouse:

- Recall times when you were younger that you remember as being fun or funny. What were those times like for you when you were a kid? What about with your spouse before your marriage? What was fun? What was funny to you?
- What humorous or funny things have you observed children doing (your own or others' children) during the last few weeks? Why do these seem funny to you? Do they seem funny to your spouse? Why or why not?
- Why were the children having fun? What were they doing? What was the result of "having fun" on the other children around them?
- Having fun must have been part of your mutual attraction during your courtship and dating. Recall and discuss your pre-wedding fun time together.
- What do you do now as a couple to have fun? What role does having a sense of humor play in your relationship with your spouse?

A word of caution here. We are not advocating that all play and no work leads to a good marriage relationship or to an ideal marriage partner. It is true that a few adults "never grow up." But their ongoing and extreme inappropriate and chronic immature playful behaviors interfere with their ability to be an appropriate adult and can lead to divorce and other problems.

Ideas for Adding Humor and Laughter to Your Relationship

Below are some specific ideas of ways you can increase humor and laughter in your life. Giving specific instructions on how to increase humor at home is a daunting task. Humor is rarely constrained to be on command or to work within a timetable. It would be like meeting a comedian at a party and saying to her, "Say something funny!" When the pressure is on to be funny, it usually backfires. But humor and playfulness are an attitude that can be developed and enhanced.

Make Time with Your Sweetheart the #1 Priority in Your Life

We live in a society that over-schedules everyone's time, and yet we wonder why we are suffering from an epidemic of stress-related illnesses. Before taking on additional duties or hobbies, ask yourself, "How will this affect the time I have with my marriage or family?" Learn how to say no to additional commitments that would unduly cramp your time. Or learn to give up something or adapt so that you will not erode your time with your spouse. You will then protect the time you have with your sweetheart. Humor and laughter happen much easier in the context of *quantity time,* and if we are not careful, quantity and quality time with our spouse will be less and less.

Be Flexible

When you are doing a chore or task and your partner starts flirting with you or teasing you, return fire! A couple of minutes enjoying each other isn't going to put your life off schedule. On the other hand, by pushing your partner away because you "need to get this finished" can potentially cause hurt feelings. Being flexible enough that you can recognize, adapt, and respond with fun and humor when you are in a teasing or joking moment can strengthen your connection with each other. This is a tremendous skill to develop. Pay attention to the following ideas:

- Gain awareness. Initially, you will be able to recognize those moments after they happen. Don't beat yourself up about missed opportunities. Learn from them. See if there is a pattern to them. A pattern is simply if the same situation happens more than once.

- Play it out in your mind. After you have identified a pattern, decide how you would like to respond. Go over your desired scenario several times in your head. Imagine yourself in that situation. Rehearse it in your mind.

- Commit to your desired response. Commit yourself to attempt the kind of response you want to give the next time the situation comes up. But don't be rigid in your expectations. Remember, the goal is to have flexible fun.

- Just do it! Take the risk and try your intended or desired response and see what happens. It may catch your partner a bit off guard the first couple of times. Don't worry; your spouse will be pleasantly surprised.

Be the First to Laugh at Yourself

If you are able to laugh at yourself, you will put everyone around you at ease. Life can be serious enough without you taking yourself so seriously on top of it. One temptation when laughing at yourself is to put yourself down. It can be humorous to say, "I was such an idiot," or "How smart was that?" Use caution when using this kind of language. Doing this is not a good idea because it may injure your sense of worth or esteem.

Another way to free yourself so that you are able to laugh at yourself is to remember that your spouse loves you for you. He or she knows the *real* you! Having faith in your partner's unconditional love makes it safer to find humor in your life. Make sure you are returning the favor in giving your sweetheart the same love and respect.

GET TO KNOW YOUR PARTNER'S PREFERENCES

Over time you will learn when you can laugh *with* your sweetheart. Never laugh *at* your spouse. Many of you have probably learned the hard way about what you can and cannot laugh about with your partner. It takes time and experience to learn those things, so be patient with each other. Take time to sit down with your spouse and answer the following questions together.

- What do you find funny?
- Is there any overlap between what you find funny and what your spouse does?
- What did you laugh about, or find humorous, during your dating life?
- How has your sense of humor changed over time?
- How has your partner's sense of humor changed over time?

If you have found a similar funny bone between the two of you, great! Most couples do have some "secrets" or codes that convey their humor with each other. Do your best to make that kind of humor a part of your life on a regular basis. Do some of the things you enjoyed during dating and engagement. Create a scrapbook of some of your funniest moments together. Don't forget to try new activities. How long has it been since you've been on a group date? Trying new things can bring you closer together.

Cautions Regarding Humor

If you have found that you both enjoy sarcasm, use it with caution. Sarcasm by definition is incongruent communication. In other words, you say one thing, but mean another. Usually, the words are positive ("that was smart"), but the intended meaning is completely different ("that was stupid"). When things are going well, bantering and teasing has its place.

But sarcasm can quickly get out of hand and lead to hurt feelings when it takes a biting tone. Sarcasm lends itself to underlying anger seeping through. Once someone's feelings are hurt, the incongruent nature of sarcasm can cause misunderstandings and a lot of "I didn't mean that" apologies later. To sum up, if you enjoy sarcasm, use with caution and make sure your sweetheart is in the mood to play along.

In all types of humor, spouses and family members should be careful not to offend, intimidate, or embarrass each other. We should laugh with rather than at another person. No one likes to be the brunt of a joke or be teased. One of the saddest and most inappropriate interactions that we occasionally see is when a person makes fun of his or her spouse in a pubic setting. This is never appropriate. Humor can hurt as well as heal.

Two Big Complaints

Here we attempt to address two of the leading complaints that individuals have about their partners when it comes to humor in marriage. We've also offered suggestions of what to do about these situations.

COMPLAINT #1 : MY PARTNER IS NEVER SERIOUS.

Life is full of things that are serious. Yet, there is a time and place for fun and play as well as a time for being serious. Our concern is that the majority of life has become filled with things that "need" to be done or "needed to be done yesterday." This attitude can become so much a part of a marital script that there doesn't ever seem to be a good time or place to play—that is, to have fun together.

If you think that your partner is never serious, be careful not to go to the other extreme to balance out or compensate for your partner. This is a common dynamic that happens with couples. A spouse will perceive that his or her partner is too far one way on a certain behavior, value, or expectation. So, in order to balance things out, the other spouse will take up the opposite side of the behavior, value or expectation. Doing this will create a large obstacle in your relationships and deny you the moderate ground that you desire. So if you think your partner is never serious, and they want to have fun and laugh at an appropriate time, *have fun with them!* Don't deny yourself an enjoyable time to prove a point. That benefits no one.

One way around this obstacle is to schedule extra time for the things that "need" to be done. You will then have some flexibility to laugh and have fun without constantly feeling constrained by the external factors in your life. One final question for you. Is it possible that you could learn how to find humor in life from your fun-loving partner?

COMPLAINT #2: My partner is ALWAYS serious.

As was previously mentioned, there is a time and place for fun and play. There are also times that require you to be more serious. If you find yourself consistently trying to get your partner to "lighten up" or "loosen up," you are probably being accused of never being serious. Do you find yourself trying to get your partner to have fun even if it would be a time you would normally be serious?

If you answered yes, you may be falling into the same trap of moving to an opposite extreme to balance out your partner. Do your best to be serious when you would normally be serious. Have fun and find humor where you normally would. One parting question for you as well. Is it possible that you could learn how to be more serious at certain times from your sweetheart?

The Joy of the Inside Joke

One of the clearest signs of the power of humor in relationships is the "inside joke." All it takes is a knowing look, smirk, or a simple phrase to get both people laughing. An inside joke in your marriage is something that just you two share. No one else knows what is going on. Even if you explained it to others, they won't appreciate it the same way you do. The inside joke binds the two of you together and marks you as a couple to others. It also is a wonderful sort of shared intimacy that defines the uniqueness of your relationship.

You can create the opportunity for inside jokes to bind you together with two ingredients—time and shared experiences. The more time you spend together, the greater the chance that you will create inside jokes.

Love, Laugh, and Live

Learn to see the humor in your marriage as you enjoy your time together. Give yourself and your partner permission to laugh and find humor in life. A great example of the power of humor is through a miserable experience, for example a camping trip. Imagine the not-so-funny rainstorm that you survived in that wet tent and sleeping bag in the mud and cold. Weeks or months later when you look at the pictures (real or imagined) of that ordeal, some of it turns into funny events and stories. These stories get better with retelling and as time passes. What was a drizzle at the time of the camping trip can evolve into a downpour with time. If you're a storyteller, it may become "the worst storm seen in 20 years!" The result is that you now have a shared experience that may have seemed negative at the time, but is fun and funny to look back on. And the magic is that you are now bonded; your marriage is strengthened with that shared experience and recollection.

Humor is good for your physical and psychological health. It will also create vitality, excitement, and an intimate connection between the two of you that keeps your marital embers smoldering.

CHAPTER 21

"What's the DIF": Growth and Change in Your Marriage

THE KEY: Recognizing and appreciating growth and change in your relationship, yourself, and in your spouse, can help strengthen your marriage.

We are all changing, all of the time. Even the cells in your body are being replaced so that you are literally a different person every seven to ten years. Growth and change is a natural part of life.

As a married couple you have a choice: you can accept the fact that change is happening or you can run from it or ignore it. Notice that we say, *accept that change is happening* rather than *accept changes*. Some changes that occur are probably not for the best.

Take for example Nate's waistline. It has steadily increased over the past four years to the point it has its own nickname. Nate can ignore the change, downplay it, or pretend that it isn't happening. If he chooses to do that, he most likely will continue his eating habits and lack of exercise. This is akin to just "accepting change." His thoughts go something like this, "This is just who I am and where I am in life. I just need to deal with it." These thoughts have a close cousin, in reference to others, "This is just who I am so *they* need to live with it."

The "live with it" and "deal with it" lines are typically used when we are on the defensive or are trying to justify a behavior or attitude that we, or our spouse, find hurtful or offensive. In those times when our guard is down, most of us readily admit that we would like to change those very things that we have told ourselves and others, "That is who I am, if you don't like it . . ." This situation shows up over and over again in our clinical work. When individuals feel safe and have no need to defend or justify, they are more open to admit their shortcomings and identify what changes they would like to make. Admitting that you need to make a change is a psychologically vulnerable position to be in, and it is in this vulnerable place that married couples can create intimacy.

A couple we'll call Marcel and Lydia had been coming for therapy to help them work through some sexual issues. This was the first marriage for both and they had found each other in their late 20s. They each had successful careers and had navigated the transition to marriage beautifully with the exception of this one area. Their main complaint was in reference to the frequency they wanted to have intercourse. Marcel stated at the beginning of counseling that he had "a high sex drive." He said, "I could have sex every day and it would just barely be enough. She used to be like me before we got married."

Lydia responded, "He's right. I did enjoy sex a lot more then than I do now. At least then we were doing some other activities besides just sex. Now that's all he wants. That's all he talks about. That's all he thinks about and it is driving me nuts! It's like someone has hit a "turn off" switch in me. I want nothing to do with sex at this point. I could probably tolerate it once a month if Marcel would just stop whining and complaining so much."

During individual interviews, when their spouse wasn't in the room, Marcel *and* Lydia each said something like, "I would love to make love with my spouse." They each said that having sex "once or twice a week" would be their ideal. Marcel and Lydia's ideals were actually much closer to each other than they thought. Yet they each were afraid to give up their stated positions ("nonstop sex" versus "as little as possible").

Marcel and Lydia's relationship didn't start off this way. Their relationship was good enough that they each felt strongly that marriage was a good idea and what they wanted. They had then—and still had—a lot of things going for them. They naturally used many of the marital keys discussed in this book to gain an understanding of each other and their own desires when it came to the sex issue. They came up with some plans of what they wanted to have happen in their relationship. It is at this point that "What's the DIF?" came into play for them.

DIF stands for:

Duration: Duration indicates the length of *time* a certain behavior, emotion, or interaction occurs. A verbal fight may last fifteen minutes or five days. Either way, there is a specific time period associated with *one* incident. We would hope that the *duration* of their verbal fight about sex would drop significantly over time. Often couples are very good at "keeping score" or track of the duration of fights and unpleasant interactions. Though less often done, a couple could also track the duration of positive interactions, for example, "we talked lovingly for two hours last night."

Intensity: Intensity can be visualized as a way of describing the strength of feelings. Intensity can be assessed on a scale of 1-10 with "10" being the most intense and "1" being the least intense. Intensity at a "10" can be excellent if that is referring to such things as loving feelings, positive interactions, and intimacy. However, a "10" on intensity can also refer to painful or difficult emotions and experiences such as depression, arguments, and hurt. An intensity rating of "1" or "2" stands for low levels of intensity. When applied to loving feelings, positive interaction, and intimacy, this low rating is very undesirable. A low intensity rating of a "1" or "2" on negative feelings of depression and pain is good news.

Frequency: Frequency refers to how often an event occurs. "Events" can be emotions, feelings, and/or interactions and behaviors that you experience individually or as a couple. Frequency can refer to how often you have disagreements, or how many times you kiss. Depending on the aspect of your relationship you are trying to describe and track, frequency may be the number of events that occur over the course of a day, week, month, or even years.

By themselves duration, intensity, and frequency (DIF) are not "good" or "bad." They just are. Each aspect of DIF is inherently without value or meaning. The value of DIF is that it can be useful as a way to help identity and keep track of how feelings and behaviors are changing in your relationship, or individually.

Here are some basic things to keep in mind when using DIF:

Pick one type of interaction, feeling, or issue that you want to track. The more specific, the better. For Marcel and Lydia, it was frequency of sex. Another way to think about this is to try to track "symptoms" rather than the "illness." So, for Marcel and Lydia they tracked the frequency of sex rather trying to track a low or high sex drive.

We know that being in love is not an illness! Then again, some signs of illness such as a queasy stomach, light-headedness, sweating, shallow breathing, and a racing heart are also common signs of the early stages of love. You each have identifiable "symptoms" that show you are in love with your spouse. For example, you might observe how far apart you stand or sit when you talk. Couples that tend to like each other are comfortable face to face about 18 inches apart when they are having a relaxed discussion. They are comfortable being so close. On the other hand, just imagine a co-worker getting that close to have a discussion!

Another example of trying to track the "symptoms" rather than the "illness," is if you decided to track exercising together rather than trying to track "getting healthy." Exercising is a "symptom" of getting healthier. You could separately track other indicators of getting healthier, like eating healthy lunches and dinners or taking vitamins.

You can use "what's the DIF" in many ways. You can use it to track decreases in undesirable feelings, behavior, and interactions or to track increases in those same areas. We recommend that you use "What's the DIF?" to track the increasing signs that your relationship is moving in a desired direction. This is a powerful tool that we'll discuss more.

Critical Concept 1

People tend to drift toward what they are focusing on. Take for example the familiar phrase "you are what you eat." Or the statement attributed to Dale Carnegie, "If you want to be enthusiastic, act enthusiastic." Even notice when you are driving your car. As you look out to your left, which way does the car tend to drift? People become what they are focused on. This is true in the psychological, emotional, and relational aspects of our lives.

Here is a little exercise to try. The goal of this exercise is to NOT think about white polar bears. Go ahead, do you best to NOT think about white polar bears. Don't think about the North Pole. Don't think about certain cola commercials at Christmastime. Don't think about bears in general. Don't think about winter or snow. Don't think about anything white!

Perhaps it might help to go back into your childhood and try to determine why you're thinking about white polar bears so much. In fact, wasn't it your mother and father who loved polar bears so much and put all those pictures of polar bears in your house while you were growing up? Who couldn't have come out of that environment without a serious case of PBP? That stands for Polar Bear Problem. See the self-help section of your local bookstore if this sounds familiar. Yes, your parents are definitely to blame for your polar bear problem. Now that you have figured out the source of your polar bear problem, you should be able to stop thinking about white polar bears, right?

So, how did you do? Were you able to achieve your goal of not thinking about white polar bears? No, of course not. Don't worry; you are not alone. By focusing on what you wanted to avoid, you actually were being drawn toward it. You may be thinking that the solution to the polar bear problem is simple—just think about anything else. Think about Hawaii. Think about warm sandy beaches with a cool breeze coming in over the top of the waves crashing on shore. Think about the sun gently warming your face as you spy the perfect hammock strapped to two coconut trees whose sole purpose of existence is to support your hammock. (No polar bear thoughts right? Okay, maybe now that we brought it up again. . . .)

The intriguing piece of all of this is that when we want to make changes in our lives, we tend to gravitate toward finding out *why* we are having problems. There is a legitimate place for having some understanding of how you got to the point you are in your life. As soon as you have an idea of where you are and how you got there, the burden of changing shifts 100 percent to you and your partner.

But it is so easy to blame others instead of taking responsibility for yourself. If you blame, you are actually giving up your power to change because you are now waiting for the other person to make the change. After all, it's their fault, right? It is their fault, it's their problem, and therefore their responsibility to change. Are you willing to put your goals and dreams to the side and just sit by and wait for them to change? When you blame, that is exactly what is happening.

So instead of focusing on what you don't want to be happening in your life, or blaming others, try to focus on the positive change you want in your life. Focus on what you *do want* rather than what you *do not want*. Again, you will tend to drift to where your focus is. If you want to stop thinking about polar bears, you should instead try thinking about something else—really anything else—because you can't think about two things at the same time. Hawaii is incompatible with polar bears. This is why we recommend that you find positive aspects of your relationship to focus on instead of focusing on getting rid of negative aspects.

Here is a final example. If you are consciously working on listening and trying to understand and validate you partner, you are not likely to get defensive. Trying to show empathy is incompatible with being defensive. Many couples might say, "We want to stop arguing." A therapist might respond with, "Okay, then what will you be doing with all of your free time now that you won't be arguing?" The couple is then encouraged to focus on identifying and implementing what they will be doing rather than what they won't be doing (arguing). Since there is only so much time for interaction, if that time is positive, there is little or no time for negative interaction.

Critical Concept 2

Don't compare your relationship to other relationships. Do your best not to compare your relationship to your neighbors, even if doing so makes you seem to feel better. Also stay away from media portrayals of what marriage is "supposed" to be like. When gathering information on marriage, do your homework, check credentials, ask for references.

You are the experts on your relationship. You are the master architects to design and build your marriage. You got married because you had what you thought was a good plan. Recall and rediscover what has worked the best for you and your marriage thus far. One of the best ways to find what works in your relationship is to compare your relationship now to your past relationship with each other.

Once you have picked a positive aspect of your relationship you want to increase and track, ask yourself, "What's the DIF between where we are now and where we were six months ago?" We recommend that you use a 3- to 6-month window for most aspects of marriage. The only exception to that is if your relationship is having a difficult time. Then, focusing on how you are changing and growing as a couple on a weekly basis can be beneficial. We are always changing as individuals and in our relationships. We will be growing and changing on at least one aspect of the DIF.

Duration, intensity, and frequency are related topics. At the same time, they are separate and unique. Let's go back to Marcel and Lydia for a moment. Marcel and Lydia decided that they each wanted to create more time and energy for sex by going out on dates, doing nonsexual activities out of the home, and with good old-fashioned romance. So with this proactive goal in mind, they asked themselves, "What is the DIF in our dating lately as to where we were three months ago?"

They found that three months ago, their dates lasted only an hour or two (duration). On an enjoyment scale of 1-10 (intensity), they were about a 3 for Lydia and a 5 for Marcel (about a 2 for him if sex didn't follow). These dates were happening about once a month (frequency). They now have a baseline to rate themselves with from this point on.

As two successful professionals, they were able to schedule their dates to twice a month. This represents a small and positive change in the frequency of the dates. At first the intensity did not change much, nor the duration for that matter. However, there was a positive change occurring in the frequency aspect. They also made an attempt to vary the location and type of dates they went on. The dates were specifically about togetherness and not a prelude to the bedroom. Over the next six months, the duration and intensity of their dates improved and the frequency went back to once a month. Yet if you asked Marcel and Lydia, they would be ecstatic because they each rated their last date at an "8" and the date lasted for 3 to 4 hours (We'll let you guess what happens after a date that was rated an "8").

We realize that asking you to try "What's the DIF?" may be awkward at first. But you may not realize that you probably are already doing it in some form. It is the same type of conversation that goes something like this (imagine you are on a date):

> You: "Remember that year after our little Pat was born?"
>
> Your Sweetheart: "Yeah, I remember. I'm glad we have Pat, but I wouldn't want to repeat that first year. We went out, what . . . maybe four times that whole year?"
>
> You: (laughing) "Yeah, that was about it. Those dates weren't much to write home about. I swear we were almost asleep at the restaurant."
>
> Your Sweetheart: (laughing too) "We completely forgot about romance; we were dreaming of uninterrupted sleep at that point."
>
> You: "I'm sure glad we get out more now."
>
> Your Sweetheart: "Me too. It's nice to be out and have a decent steak without worrying if I was going to end up using the steak for a pillow. How long until we need to get back to relieve the sitter?"

Putting numbers and specifics to these types of conversations just formalizes and gives a bit more focus to what you normally do. It is consciously tracking the growth and change in your relationship. Some couples will put notes or symbols on a calendar or planner so they can see how they are changing. They may have something like "D=2 hours; I=8" on a day they had an event they were tracking. You will see frequency as you look at the calendar and the number of events add up over the course of time. If anyone else looks at the calendar, they won't know what the symbols mean—just you and your spouse will know.

While you are increasing desired behavior, it would be helpful to give yourselves some extra rewards along the way. An extra special dinner, romantic weekend getaway, breakfast in bed, can all be ways in which you reward yourselves for progress. What rewards would work well for you? Eventually, the changes will become a reward in and of themselves.

Here are some vital points to remember from this chapter. Implementing these things in your relationship is a key to helping it improve and grow.

- We are always changing as individuals and in our marriage.
- We tend to drift to where our focus is. (Avoid the Polar Bear Problem!)
- It is better focus on what we want in our marriage than what we want to get rid of.
- Compare your marriage to yourselves and no one else.
- Ask yourselves, "What's the DIF?" to find specific evidence of growth and progress.
- D=duration (time in hours, days, weeks, months, and so on).
- I=intensity (scale 1-10).
- F=frequency (per day, week, or month).
- Calendar or chart your DIF progress over time.
- Reward yourselves for your progress.

CHAPTER 22
Marriage and Physical Health

THE KEY: By making your marriage a priority, you set the foundation of success, health, and happiness in the other areas of your life.

What you put into, and do with, your body affects your health. This is a no-brainer for most of us. However, finding the motivation to exercise and have a healthy diet is a different story. Increasingly, researchers are finding links between people's health and their *social* environment. That's right, their *social* environment. The quality and strength of your relationships with your spouse, family, and friends can affect your physical health for better or for worse.

People with strong ties to their sweetheart and family enjoy the following health benefits when compared to people with poor-quality relationships:

- Less heart disease
- Longer life
- Fewer doctor visits
- Fewer hospitalizations
- Greater wealth

270

• Deeper social support network

Strong marital and emotional support is connected to better health. The opposite is also true: when you are depressed, anxious, or experiencing difficult marital or familial interactions, your health suffers. When your health suffers, you go to the doctor more, and you may be more accident-prone because you're preoccupied. More health problems mean more money spent on health care and, therefore, less on preferred expenditures.

More than three decades of research show that people who seek counseling for psychological and emotional issues visit the doctor *less* often after counseling! Fewer visits to the doctor equals less money spent on health care. Of course, these people have to pay for psychotherapy in place of other medical bills, but after six to eight months of therapy (six to twelve sessions); the overall savings can start to kick in.

Other fascinating research shows that when a couple or family attends therapy, on average, *everyone* in the family makes fewer doctor visits. Not only are our minds and bodies intricately connected, but we are connected to those close to us. Research in the past decade has shown that when Mom and Dad take care of their psychological, physical, and emotional health, their children tend to have a better quality of life as well.

Stress Hormones and Health

What explains the link between mind and body? The simple answer is stress. Stress generates a psychological and physical reaction simultaneously. Sometimes the physical stress reaction happens before we recognize it. Sometimes it is the other way around. Regardless of which comes first, the result is the same. The body receives a rush of a special hormone called cortisol, which starts a cascade of chemical reactions that increase blood pressure and heart rate. The nervous system goes on alert, and the senses are heightened. The immune system actually begins to shut down as the rest of the body prepares to fight or flee. The process is similar to revving a car engine in preparation for a drag race.

In the face of physical danger—a daily occurrence anciently—people needed this response to help preserve their life. Imagine turning a corner to find yourself face-to-face with a lion. The cascade of stress hormones would give you a chance to fight the lion or get the heck out of there. Once you were safe, the stress reaction would abate and your body would return to normal. Your engine would return to regular idling.

Thankfully, lions don't lurk around every corner in this day and age. But if you did meet a lion, the choices would be clear—run away or become dinner. Our world is also very stressful; we may not worry about real lions, but we face lion-like situations every day. Bosses, bills, traffic, school, work, and relationships can cause the same engine-revving stress reaction as meeting a lion.

Unless you are careful, your stress reactions can become constant, never allowing stress hormones to return to normal levels. Imagine revving your car engine nonstop. The engine would wear out quickly, as would most of the systems connected to the engine. Your body is no different: prolonged exposure to cortisol and the chemical reactions it is linked to lead to high blood pressure, arterial disease, increased susceptibility to illness, and so on.

Cavemen went to work when the sun came up and went home when it got dark, *whenever* it got dark. At night, they hung out in the cave with their buddies. They didn't necessarily have to go hunting every day. A big kill could feed a lot of people for a couple days. They worked when necessary and rested when necessary. No daily schedules (beyond that of the sun) dictated their routine. We can learn a lesson from cavemen.

The lesson is that a stressor is not a stressor unless it is *perceived* to be a stressor. Perception is a huge factor in determining the extent of the cortisol cascade, or the stress reaction. Some people drive in traffic and perceive it as a lion. Others see it as a mild inconvenience, or even an opportunity. How you *perceive* the situation greatly affects how your body responds. Those rose-colored glasses can come in handy!

Even if you're a realist (or a pessimist) you can change your responses to stressful situations. When faced with a situation—say, traffic—try to come up with a few ways the situation can be helpful in the short or long run. You probably have a gift for solving problems because you perceive almost every situation as a problem. Do your heart and health a favor by getting in the habit of looking *a bit* more on the bright side. You don't have to become a Pollyanna; that would require you to give up your greatest strength. However, by identifying and dwelling on some possible positive outcomes, you'll establish a healthy psychological balance. Healthy perceptions lead to decreased stress, which leads to better physical health.

Serenity Now

Just saying "serenity now" may not do too much for your stress level, but trying to relax in potentially stressful situations is a great idea. This ability is best achieved through a lot of practice. High levels of anxiety, stress, and anger were enemies to a samurai because they prevented him from focusing and responding effectively. So, the samurai began their training with easy skills and rehearsed them endlessly until they could perform these skills without conscious thought. Stress management techniques are no different.

One powerful technique to help diminish stress is "letting go" of things over which you have no power, like traffic. The Serenity Prayer used by most twelve-step programs creates an appropriate mind-set: "God grant me the courage to change the things I can, the serenity to accept the things I can't, and the wisdom to know the difference." For example, when you're stuck in traffic, use the time to listen to a book on tape or to plan the next day's schedule so when you do get home, you can be there psychologically and emotionally as well.

The secret to letting go is simple: focus on what you *can* do rather than what you *can't* do. Many people create stress in their lives by focusing on what they *should* be doing, or what they think their life *should* be like. Living a "should-y" life keeps them from living a life rich in possibilities.

Time-Out

Keeping a positive focus is particularly helpful during a potentially stressful situation. Taking a regular "time-out" to rejuvenate your mind, body, and soul is a crucial step toward handling stressful situations.

Think of your stress level on a scale from one to ten. One represents very little stress, while ten may feel like you're having a heart attack. Regular relaxation will help you stay on the lower end of the scale. Life throws curveballs—some straight at your head. Each stressful event in life can have a point value.

For example, your spouse's returning home late from work may rate a point value of two, meaning that your stress level increases by two points. If you haven't taken time for yourself to relax, and your stress level is already percolating at a five, this event will bump it up to a seven. When your spouse walks in the door, your voice and body language may be agitated. Now, if your spouse had a difficult day or got stuck in traffic, she may be fuming around a five or six herself. When she receives a less-than-warm reception, her stress level may also increase. With both partners experiencing moderate to high stress levels, an event like getting home late from work can easily turn into an ugly confrontation.

Now imagine that you have been taking time regularly to rejuvenate, and your stress level is around a one when your spouse is late. The event still bumps up your stress level two points, to a three on the scale. When your spouse comes home, your greeting may be less snappy. Just for fun, imagine that your spouse used the time she spent in the traffic jam to work through the day's issues and plan tomorrow's schedule, enabling her to "leave work at the office." This will allow for a very different homecoming. You may feel concern or perhaps just mild agitation. Your spouse may explain the delay and apologize without becoming defensive. The homecoming may be a stress reliever rather than a stressor. Each party has a responsibility toward the homecoming. By managing their own internal stressors, the partners are able to help each other rather can causing each other more stress.

Prolonged stress is toxic to your body and relationships. Taking time for rest and relaxation is crucial for both your physical and relational health. Some people have a difficult time finding interests or activities that help them feel rejuvenated. Everyone is a little different—some people feel rejuvenated after doing active things like sports; others recharge their batteries through physically passive means, such as meditating, reading, or watching movies. Still others find that being with people in a social setting, especially close friends or family members, helps them relax.

If you struggle with finding an interest, try the following exercise:

(1) Get a pencil and paper and go to a local bookstore that has an extensive magazine rack. Allow at least one hour for this exercise.

(2) Start looking through the magazines. If a magazine's front-page content (not the attractive model on the cover) jumps out at you, pick up the magazine and flip through it. You don't have to buy it.

(3) Write down the title or focus of the magazine on your paper and then move to the next magazine that grabs your attention.

(4) Do not ignore magazines that jump out at you just because someone you know might not approve. This activity is to help you find *your* interests, not someone else's.

Illness and Stress

Up to this point, we have discussed how healthy relationships can have a positive effect on physical health. But life inevitably includes illnesses, and we have to work through them. Illness can greatly impact a relationship. However, healthy relationships can help diminish many effects of illness. When illness does occur in a marital or family situation, everyone's perception of the illness will determine its effect on the family.

One of the first things you can do to fight the effects of illness on your marriage or family is to rally the troops. Your friends and extended family network are critical. Not only can they support the ill person, but they can also support the supporters. Having someone to lean on has tremendous power.

Some people feel that they don't have anyone to turn to. If you feel isolated or do not have a large support network, you can still do many things. Activity in religious organizations, clubs, or support groups can expand that critical social support network. If you're shy or reserved, consider letting an acquaintance help you branch out a bit. You have value, and not only will others willingly reach out to help you, but you will have a chance to enrich their lives as well.

The second thing you can do is to find out others' (spouse's and children's, specifically) perspectives and feelings about the illness. Try to talk about the illness rather than the person; avoid attaching the sickness to the individual with phrases such as "Sally's cancer," or "Johnny's depression." Rather it should be "the cancer," or the depression Johnny is dealing with." Talking about the illness as if it were separate from your loved one is a great way to support each other in the battle against the illness. The battle is not against you or your loved one struggling with the illness. By openly discussing the topic, you can address the fears that may be associated with the illness. Often, once a fear has been spoken, it loses its power.

Once the illness is discussed, the focus can shift to the prognosis. Some illnesses, such as traumatic head injuries and paralysis, cause permanent changes in ability or functioning. Serious illnesses may create a reality that is much different from what you had planned. In situations where your dreams become impossible due to your own or a loved one's illness, grieving is appropriate and very helpful. By grieving the loss of the dream, you become able to move on and to focus on other possibilities and new dreams.

Marital Health Pyramid

Grieving together is never fun, but it can bind the two of you together. Below are tips to help you be there for each other during difficult times. Frequently, a period of struggle with illness becomes a turning point for couples. They find strengths and positive traits in each other that they would not have discovered without the struggle.

Ideally, your marriage will be in a strong position before life throws a curveball at you. Below is a Marital Health Pyramid—complete with recommended daily doses of attributes and activities—that will help you create a stronger marriage. The concepts on the pyramid are briefly

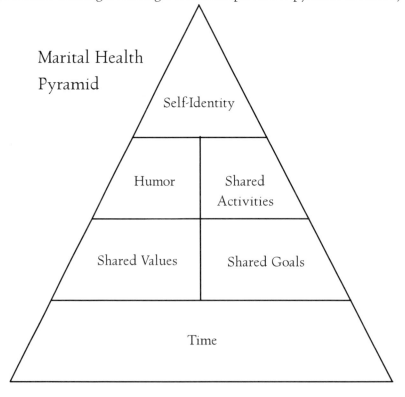

Marital Health Pyramid

Self-Identity

Humor

Shared Activities

Shared Values

Shared Goals

Time

discussed in this chapter and significantly added upon in the other chapters in this book.

This pyramid is designed to help you create a sense of emotional and physical safety in your relationship. If you feel safe, you're more likely to feel relaxed and at peace. Feeling relaxed and at peace is the antidote to stress and all the nasty side effects that prolonged stress can create.

TIME

At the base of the pyramid is the foundation of it all, *Time!* You need lots of it! Scheduling quality time is difficult, but quality time typically occurs within quantity time. Make sure you schedule *quantity time* with your sweetheart. Work schedules can be rigid, so time with your partner usually comes out of your discretionary time. The activities you choose during your discretionary time often reflect your priorities and your values; people make time for what they view as important. If you value your relationships, are you making time for them?

SHARED VALUES AND GOALS

Next on the pyramid is *Shared Values and Goals*. Values, or beliefs, determine the rules by which people make decisions and live their lives. Whenever we do something against our values, we feel an accompanying sense of guilt or remorse. Values include principles such as respect of self and others, honesty, and commitment. Our most deeply held values impact our lives the most. Partners with similar core values are the most compatible. How do you get to know your partner's values? Spend time together.

Spending time together also helps couples gain a good sense of each other's goals. Again, similar goals usually mean greater compatibility.

Similar goals as a couple provide a common purpose for spouses to work toward together. Couple-goals can deal with family size, finances, retirement plans, and so on. Set long-term goals first, and then work back to short-term goals. Short-term goals ideally lead to the achievement of long-term goals.

Shared Activities and Humor

The next step on the pyramid is *Shared Activities and Humor*. Below is a list of activities. You and your spouse should separately circle five activities that you would like to do with your sweetheart. Then share your responses with each other. Don't worry if you have never done some of these things together. The point is that you learn something more about yourself and your partner.

Typically, men enjoy doing physical activities with their partner, for example, hiking, biking, or other sports (participating or watching). Women generally enjoy activities that provide a psychological and emotional connection like going out to dinner, walking in the park, or turning off the TV and just talking about the day, and your hopes, goals, dreams, and desires.

Running/Walking	Going Out to Dinner
Going to a Movie	Playing Golf
Fishing	Going to an Art Show or Museum
Worshiping Together	Camping Hunting
Attending a Seminar	Going to the Theatre
Attending a Concert	Snuggling
Relaxing at Home	Attending a Marriage Retreat
Reading a Self-Help Book	Exercising or Working Out

Humor occupies the same level as Shared Activities on the Marital Health Pyramid. A good sense of humor—especially the ability to laugh at yourself—can dissipate the most tense situations. Research shows that humor is the number-one technique used to relieve tension and avoid explosions in arguments. But humor must be used wisely; making fun of your spouse or using sarcasm can be toxic to your relationship.

A good rule of thumb is to follow your partner's lead. For example, a father and his adult son were fishing together. As the father walked across a large log that spanned the slow-moving river, he started to slip. Trying to regain his balance and stay dry, the father started to flail his arms. As if he were in slow motion, he hit the water with a satisfying splash. Standing up, he sputtered a bit and looked sheepishly at his son, who was standing on the shore. The son looked at his dad with a smirk and said, "I need to know if you're okay so I can have permission to laugh." They both broke into laughter at this point. This story still draws a laugh when the family gets together. You can apply this same kind of reasoning to tense situations and discussions in your marriage.

INDIVIDUAL IDENTITY

Keeping your individual identity, interests, and talents is also important. Your *Individual Identity* is what made you attractive to your spouse. The opposite is also true: your sweetheart has strengths and attributes that attracted you to her. Sometimes the very behaviors and attributes that initially attracted you to each other annoy you now. Reminding yourself daily why you married your partner will help you keep a positive perspective on your spouse and your relationship.

Another way to retain your individuality while remaining connected to your spouse is to create an open and safe environment

CHAPTER 23
Your Marriage Through the Years

THE KEY: Successfully adapting to the many changes and challenges as the years go by will make your marriage great.

R ecently we heard a married couple talking together about some things that they had to do. It was not a particularly unusual conversation and went something like this. "What do you have planned on Saturday?" The spouse responded, "I was thinking that we would go to the furniture store and look for that bed that we need to buy, then make a stop at the pharmacy for the prescriptions, do the grocery shopping, and when we get home, finish getting the bedroom ready for our new arrival." The other spouse replied, "I know that we have to do those things, but also we need to work in some time to get ready for tomorrow's picnic, and I also need to spend a couple of hours mid-afternoon meeting with the neighborhood committee. How are we going to get it all done?"

What would you say might be the age of this couple? Are they newlyweds in their late twenties? A couple who had been married some fifteen years or so? Or a couple who had been married thirty-five years? In fact, could it not be true that the same conversation might have been between a husband and wife in each of the three age groups?

The newlyweds would like to go to the furniture store to look for a baby crib. Then they wanted to get home and finish painting and decorating the bedroom for their new baby who is due in two months. The grocery shopping was to get some basic items but also to purchase the main menu fixings for Sunday's picnic that they were hosting for two other couples. Part of the husband's responsibility for getting ready for the picnic was assembling the new barbecue grill he had purchased.

The couple who had been married fifteen years or so might be going to the furniture store to look for a new mattress for themselves, moving from a double bed to a king-size mattress. They needed to stop by the pharmacy to pick up a prescription for one of their children who had an inner-ear infection. Their usual pattern of grocery shopping was to have the wife do it during the week; however, they were attempting to implement a new plan of shopping together on Saturday so that they would be able to fit in a bit more time together. The "new arrival" was the king-size mattress, and they needed to remodel their bedroom so it would fit. The picnic that they needed to prepare for was one involving one of their children's sports teams and included the team members and their parents. One spouse needed to attend the neighborhood committee meeting, which was dealing with possible rezoning of the area for commercial development; this couple very much wanted to keep their area a residential neighborhood.

What about the couple who had been married for thirty-five years or so? Perhaps they were going to the furniture store to look for a hospital-type bed for one of their aging widowed mothers who was moving into their home so that they could provide appropriate care for her. The stop at the pharmacy was to pick up prescriptions, not only for themselves, but also for this aging parent. And, you guessed it: the bedroom that they were getting ready for a "new arrival" was, in fact, for the mother. Tomorrow's picnic was going to be one that they hosted at their home for their two married children and spouses, five grandchildren, the wife's parents who lived nearby, and the husband's widowed mother. Scenarios like those above are just a glimpse of the sort of changes that can occur over the years for a married couple. Successful and happy marriages are those in which the wife and husband adjust and adapt to situations as they arise. This demands flexibility, along with a commitment to the marriage and to one another's happiness.

A Life Cycle Perspective on Marriage

Most couples that we talk with who have been married for a while relate that they have been through various stages, phases, and life events together. We believe that the ability of a couple to understand and openly discuss both their changing roles and how they have coped with change over the years through their marriage is one of the keys to a healthy and happy relationship.

What follows is a description of what we term the *marital life cycle*. As you read this chapter, take time to discuss these ideas and concepts with your spouse. Does the information here coincide with your marriage experience? Does it make sense as you look into the future? How might you change the ideas and information that we have presented so that it more accurately reflects your marriage? In other words, use this as a stimulus to create and describe your own marital life cycle.

Those who study marriage and family relationships have determined that a marital or family cycle can comprise many stages.

And of course this is true, depending upon how one views and labels what is going on throughout the marital history. We have found that the marital life cycle generally encompasses four stages. The four stages we are presenting apply to couples whose marriage is not interrupted or broken by either divorce or the death of one of the spouses. However these ideas can work in understanding any marriage.

The Marital Life Cycle

Describing marital development and progression across the life cycle of your marriage can help you become more aware of how your marriage will change or has changed over time. For each of the four stages of the marital life cycle, there are five core tasks that are experienced by couples over time. These core tasks change over time and reflect the changing nature of your marriage. In great marriages, husbands and wives successfully accomplish marital developmental tasks through the efforts of both spouses in achieving their marital goals.

The four stages in the marital life cycle are:

• Stage 1—The Foundational Years: Mating and Marriage
• Stage 2—The Early Years: Building the Base
• Stage 3—The Middle Years: Affirmation and Continuation
• Stage 4—The Later Years: Consolidation and Celebration

Notice that we have not provided a specific number of years for each of the stages. It will be most useful for you, as a couple, to place yourselves into that stage in which you are currently living. Simply do this by trial and error. This process is very helpful because it will help you to apply the dynamics of these ideas to your unique relationship as you attempt to better understand and strengthen your marriage.

Within each stage of the marital life cycle stages are five core tasks or activities that couples typically accomplish. As shown below, the five core tasks are repeated in each of the four stages. Note that the achievement or accomplishment of these marital development tasks requires the efforts and involvement of both spouses. It takes both partners (two people) to build and maintain a successful marriage. Yet it takes only one spouse to destroy a marriage.

The five core tasks are:

1. Commitment: To what extent do you and your spouse value your marriage? What are your intentions with regard to working at staying married? Commitment is perhaps the most important of the tasks because marriage is the only voluntary family relationship that we have and, therefore, the most fragile.

2. Caring: How do you show genuine concern and kindness for each other?

3. Communication: How do you communicate with your sweetheart, verbally and non-verbally?

4. Conflict/Compromise: How do you recognize and deal with the inevitable differences and disagreements in your relationship?

5. Contract/Expectations: What are your expectations for your roles and your expectations for your spouse for maintaining your marriage relationship?

These core tasks will seem different and are experienced differently at various stages of the marital life cycle. Couples run into trouble when they try to achieve each task exactly same way in different stages. Flexibility, the ability to adapt to change in situations, behaviors, and attitude, is necessary over the years. The purpose of becoming aware of these marital tasks is to gain a new perspective and a broader view of your marriage relationship.

The following outline will provide you with a means to look at where you are in your Marital Life Cycle and anticipate future changes that might impact you as a married couple.

Stage 1—The Foundational Years: Mating and Marriage

During these early months and years of your relationship you establish your identity as a couple. Recall our concept discussed in other chapters that psychological marriage begins before the wedding. Marriage is a process, while a wedding is an event. Therefore, we view the foundation time of your marriage as having begun during your relationship before the wedding; that is, during your courtship. During this time you separate from your families of origin and become a married couple within your family.

In this first stage, you continue to develop the commitment to each other and to being married that prompted you to become married. Prior to your wedding you were consciously and unconsciously testing the waters to see whether there was sufficient and appropriate caring to warrant your getting married. After the wedding you learn more and more about caring, love, and compassion toward one another and from one another. Ideally, communication is very good or you wouldn't have become married! After the wedding you continue to establish workable processes and patterns to improve your communication as you build your relationship together. You have undoubtedly experienced some differences or conflict and are learning to deal with and resolve these constructively. Compromise, which is giving up something in order to gain something, likely has become one of your skills. In great marriages partners are not selfish. During this early time of your marriage, you establish a spoken and unspoken working agreement, or contract, that helps you clarify your expectations about your marriage, your roles in it, and your spouse's roles.

Stage 2—The Early Years: Building the Base

During this stage you "settle into" your marriage. Your commitment and bonding as a wife and husband deepen as you spend more time together, share experiences and get to know each other in so many ways. While there are adjustments to your marriage, your commitment is strong and becomes stronger as you experience difficulties and trials as well as wonderful times together. If children come into your marriage, this also is an event that increases commitment to each other and to your growing family. Caring also is increased as you discover new ways to show appreciation for one another. Communication is improved and strengthened as you learn more about each other. Undoubtedly, there have been increased opportunities for conflict to arise in your relationship. In great marriages, the husband and wife continue to learn to deal with conflict and reach compromises, moving their relationship into an ever-stronger and more meaningful experience. Your expectations regarding marriage and family life continue to develop on the arrival of a child. Having a child is a momentous occasion for any couple. The arrival of each new child requires the couple to clarify and re-define their expectations regarding their roles as parents. Typically, traditions and experiences regarding parenting from each spouse's family of origin come into play. Differences in parenting style and practices are discussed and worked out so that as a couple, you can suitably co-parent your children.

Stage 3—The Middle Years: Affirmation and Continuation

During this third stage you affirm that your marriage has been good for both of you. Your relationship is stronger, and you began thinking about and preparing for the remaining years.

As the years go by, you continually discover and affirm that you have weathered many experiences and developed a solid and rewarding marriage relationship. Your commitment to each other and to the idea of marriage is firm. Undoubtedly, you have friends or family members who have experienced divorce. Typically, those experiences with divorce cause a couple in their middle years to reassess the strengths of their marriage and to value the relationship that they have even more. As a couple, you have maintained a close and caring relationship in spite of divergent interests, individual needs, or issues that might threaten marital satisfaction. Communication is a core skill that improves and becomes crucial to the maintenance of your marital satisfaction.

During these middle years there may be a tendency to take one another for granted and to become lazy in communication. Partners in great marriages continually work to understand their spouse and strive to be understood. Conflict is typically decreased during these years, and happy couples learn to compromise in formal and direct ways as well as in informal and subtle ways. Role expectations and the marital bond are redefined and clarified as the couple ages and spouses progress in both personal and companionship ways. Parenting continues to be a primary role as the couple copes with the responsibility of rearing adolescents. They also learn to "love and let go" of children as they progress into post-high school years and leave home.

Stage 4—The Later Years: Consolidation and Celebration

During the fourth stage, the spouses—individually and as a married couple—attempt to achieve balance in their lives between that which they have achieved and that which they had hoped to achieve. They evaluate satisfactions and dissatisfactions. They anticipate forthcoming losses, which, for many, includes making a transition into retirement and preparing gracefully for the ending years of life

In many ways these are "golden years" for couples as they support each other and benefit from the achievements of their married years together. Commitment has been demonstrated. The couple exhibits a gratifying degree of closeness and caring during these remaining years, including demonstrations of appreciation for their shared marriage. Often the manifestations of affection and concern for one another are more visible during these years than they were during almost any time except the honeymoon! By this time spouses really do know each other, and their communication reflects this with continued verbal and nonverbal connection. Depending on age of the spouses, there can be a decrease in the couple's ability to deal constructively with conflict or to compromise with one another. It is not that the partners become selfish, but perhaps more that they are set in their ways. As we say sometimes, a spouse may experience "hardening of the categories!"

At this stage, the marital bond is very well established and understood by both partners. During this stage—or perhaps at the end of the previous stage—the expectation is that the couple's home will become an "empty nest" as children move on with their lives. However, it is not rare these days for adult children to return home to live with their parents. These children are called "boomerang kids," and they turn the "empty nest" into a "cluttered nest." Perhaps a more consistent example of how expectations change for aging couples is that spouses' bodies age and they become more limited in physical and intellectual ability, so they are forced to adapt to these realities. Growing old is difficult. One task that an increasing number of aging couples face is becoming dependent upon their adult children for ongoing care. This requires flexibility and a change in the roles of both the aging parents and their adult middle-year children (and spouses).

The Outcome

We hope that as you think about your marriage, you will be able to assess your strengths as well as areas that you wish to enhance with regard to the five core tasks we have discussed. Make this assessment for your own marriage and also for some other marriages that you are familiar with, such as your parents' marriage, your grandparents,' and others.

Not long ago we heard an elderly woman talk about her sixty-six years of marriage. She said something like, "It was more getting used to each other than working hard to change one another, which is almost impossible anyway. And after sixty-six years, I think I am finally used to him. The other day as I watched him walk across the room, I thought what an adorable little old man he has grown up to be." Perhaps that summarizes well the outcome of a happy and long married life together!

CHAPTER 24
Marriage is a Decision and Life-Style

THE KEY: Deciding to make the marriage last, and then doing it, is a key to a great marriage.

D ecisions, decisions, decisions! It seems like we spend much of our time making decisions. There are two choices: you can make a decision and stick with it, or you can make a decision and change your mind and back out of it. Today it seems that the attitude of many people entering marriage is that they can change their mind and exit the marriage. Evidence of this includes the high divorce rate and the advent of prenuptial agreements, in which, before the wedding, couples make contingencies and preparations in case they divorce. Do these attitudes and behaviors show that an engaged couple plans to stay married?

Many people believe from the outset that they will be married and divorced several times—that their first marriage will not last. A colleague of ours reported that, in a conversation, a father said in regard to his son's upcoming wedding, the bride would "make a nice first wife for Jim." Similarly, some people consider their first marriage to be a "starter marriage," implying they will divorce and marry subsequent times. We believe that the key to having a great marriage and making it last is to decide at the outset that this marriage will work. Couples entering a marriage should be committed to making their marriage work and not be concerned about or setting up some sort of legal or psychological strategies to exit from the marriage.

What did you say to each other in your wedding vows? What level of commitment to one another, and to your marriage, did you promise in them? If you can recall your vows or promises, briefly discuss them. A fairly traditional wedding vow goes something like this:

"I, (Bride/Groom), take you (Groom/Bride), to be my (husband/ wife), to have and to hold from this day forward, for better or for worse, for richer, for poorer, in sickness and in health, to love and to cherish, until death do us part."

Certainly, this vow has the ingredients of commitment.

We came across wedding vows attributed to the Book of Common Prayer from the year 1552. Of course, these vows have a religious dimension, but note particularly the last phrase:

"I take thee to have and to hold, from this day forward, for better for worse, for richer for poorer, in sickness and in health, to love and to cherish, till death due us part, according to God's holy ordinance and thereto I give thee my troth. With this ring, I thee wed, with my body I thee worship, and with all my worldly goods I thee endow."

In this vow, the couples' worldly goods, their material possessions, would be given to each other and shared in the marital relationship, with no strings attached. There was no prenuptial agreement in these vows.

Successful and happy marriages are made because the spouses decided to make their marriage last, and then they follow through with that decision. Divorce is not an option. When difficulties arise in the marriage, as occurs in every marriage, the couple works together to meet and solve those difficulties.

Beliefs about Marriage

Your beliefs about marriage are very important and influence your attitudes and behaviors. We suggest that you and your sweetheart engage in the following exercise. Read each of the statements below and then either write down or discuss your individual responses. Perhaps you could first write down your individual responses and then discuss those responses with each other in some depth. As you think about and discuss your responses, some of your beliefs may be clarified.

- I believe that a good marriage has the following characteristics...
- I decided to marry you because...
- I believe that our marriage is strong because...
- I believe that our marriage is better than others' because...
- I believe that divorce is...

As you discuss your responses, pay attention to how similar your beliefs are. You are likely to find that your beliefs and values are quite similar, which should not surprise you, because in the process of becoming psychologically married you undoubtedly have come to agree on many of your beliefs. On the other hand, your agreement may be because your beliefs about these and other marital topics were so similar that you decided to marry each other.

One of the factors that shape people's views and beliefs about marriage is the media's treatment of marriage. For many years the media has focused on the problems that marriage can create, paid undue attention to high divorce rates, and refused to acknowledge the benefits of marriage. It is human nature to focus on problems rather than strengths, to see the bad rather than the good, for this is the sort of "news" that makes headlines. Below are some questions about beliefs in marriage. Your responses may be shaped by what you have read or heard in various media.

- How do you, as husband and wife, view the purpose of marriage?
- Do you believe that marriage will work for most couples, or will *not* work for most couples?
- Do you believe that marriage is good for the partners, or that marriage is constraining and smothering for individual development?
- Does marriage make spouses happy, or does it make them miserable?
- Will marriage keep you from realizing your full potential, or will it facilitate you reaching your full potential?

What are your responses to such questions? What similar questions come to mind that you and your spouse might discuss together?

Your Commitment to Each Other

Scott Stanley and others have identified and discussed two types of commitment: commitment because of dedication and commitment because of constraint. Dedication implies devotion or attachment to another person in thoughts, feelings, and actions. Most of you have heard the song "Dedicated to the One I Love." In your marriage, dedication and commitment mean that you honor your spouse as the most important person in the world to you. Dedication involves a process of meeting that commitment to your spouse because that is your ultimate goal and wish. Dedication is about loyalty and putting your spouse as the #1 priority in your life. As the wedding vows state, dedication is "to love and to cherish" your spouse, although you may not use exactly that language in your everyday thinking or speaking.

Constraint implies commitment because of an obligation imposed by some outside force. This commitment is because "I have to" rather than "I want to." When spouses marry for the "wrong reason," the commitment to marry may have been made by constraint, an imposed, outside reason for the wedding. Such constraints can include "shotgun weddings;" the need to escape a bad family situation; feelings of, "I'm getting older and this is my last chance;" or similar circumstances. Such constraints incite very little lasting commitment to the marriage or the spouse. Rather, marriage is entered into as a means to remedy a perceived problem or frustration.

Dedication conveys the sense of a positive force drawing you forward into a marriage that you freely choose and desire. On the other hand, constraint conveys the sense of a negative force pushing you from behind into a marriage that you probably are not sure about. Most people, including men and women entering a marriage, do not like to be pushed or constrained. In fact, people don't like to be pushed or constrained at all.

Now look again at your responses to the above questions.

- Did you decide to marry your spouse because of your dedication to the idea of marriage and your dedication to him or her as a person?
- To what extent is your marriage lasting because you are dedicated to making it last, or because you are constrained or somehow coerced to stay in it?

How do you show your commitment and dedication to each other? Probably it is through many small ways that occur daily as you interact. What are special ways that you could show your love and dedication to your spouse? Recall how you showed your interest in and importance to each other during your courtship. How do you show that today? One way is to carve your initials and a heart into a tree. Trees across the land have been witness (and victim) to many romantic carvings! A similar tradition occurs on the Ponte Vecchio Bridge, a famous medieval bridge over the Arno River in Florence, Italy. Europe's oldest segmental arch bridge, it was built in 1345. In the center of the bridge is a statue honoring Florence's celebrated goldsmith, Bentvenuto Cellini. Over the years, a tradition has developed whereby lovers write or etch their names on a padlock, lock the padlock to the fence that surrounds Cellini's statue, and throw the padlock key into the river as a token of their never-to-be-broken love. We are not advocating that you deface trees or fences as a means to show your love. However, making special tokens to show your dedication and love toward each other is appropriate and fun. How about a wish in a wishing well? How else could you show your dedication to each other? What are your special tokens or acts of marital commitment?

Incidentally, so many people place padlocks on Cellini's fence on the Ponte Vecchio Bridge that the bridge caretakers must constantly cut off the locks. So onlookers see not only the fence with the many locks on it, but also the ground with broken locks and cut shackles. Observing this, one cannot help thinking that perhaps the locks on the fence represent dedicated, vibrant, lasting marriages, and the broken and cut locks on the ground represent constrained or minimally committed marriages that did not last.

Time Shows Dedication and Commitment

Commitment and dedication to the idea of marriage are both crucial. Commitment to one's spouse is also crucial for a marriage to last. A commitment is a decision. Following that decision, commitment is demonstrated by action. Thus, commitment to marriage means that spouses are dedicated to the idea of being married, and to being married to each other. They are committed to doing things to make their marriage work. A couple committed to working together to make the marriage work will have a successful and satisfying marriage and will escape the tragedy of divorce.

Your behaviors as individuals and as a married couple demonstrate the degree to which your decision to marry and maintain that commitment was final. Such a decision should be made only once. In committed marriages, abandonment or breaking up is not an option. Divorce is not an option.

How can you measure or assess your commitment to your marriage? Perhaps the simplest way to assess commitment is to look at the effort, time, and attention that you give to your marriage. We mean the time that you spend with each other when the focus can be on each other to talk about interesting things; taking a "pause that refreshes" from daily tribulations. Happily married couples give adequate time and attention to one another and to their marriage. They find time in their busy lives to do things together as wife and husband. Time together is a top priority and is scheduled and planned. Of course, the spouses do not neglect other responsibilities and obligations, yet they do not neglect marital time either.

We encourage every married couple to have a date night each week. The idea of the weekly date night is that you can look forward to and count on those hours together, protected from interference. Date night means that as a couple, you spend several hours sometime during the week in a relaxing and refreshing activity. Some find going to breakfast or lunch as a more realistic option. Of course, the date does not have to be focused on a meal. Taking walks together or doing other activities that you enjoy is what you should make time to do. At lease once during the week, put your marital relationship first. You can spend the time in unlimited ways; the point is to make your time together a priority.

As much as possible, your weekly date needs to be protected from all other interferences. Some true emergencies will arise, particularly if you are in the child-rearing years. In those instances, you should reschedule uninterrupted couple time so as not to lose it. Time lost can never be recovered. A wife will never believe she is the most important person in her husband's life until he has shown her that he is willing to keep his time commitments to her. The same is true for a husband. He needs to be shown that he is a priority in his wife's life. Actions speak louder than words.

Happily married couples find time to get away together. It doesn't matter if these are day outings, overnight stays, or longer trips. What is important is for you to have time together in a setting that is different from your daily routine. The goal is to spend time together and renew your marital relationship, as well as to rest and reflect on the blessings and challenges of life. How often should these getaways occur? That is for each couple to decide. The frequency of these getaways may vary over the years, but it is important that they occur.

You Married a Family

Once children enter the marriage, things change! One of the things that can change is the added opportunity to have a weekly family council or family evening, in which some time is set aside during each week in which family members get together for fun, fellowship, and planning. The family can play games, tell stories, plan for vacations or other activities, coordinate schedules, or do almost anything else. This family council time, regularly scheduled, improves communication and demonstrates commitment to one another—both parent to child and sibling to sibling.

It is also important for couples to be involved in extended family activities and relationships. This is true whether you have children or not. Of course, parents become involved—possibly to the point of fatigue—in supporting their children in school and other activities. But parents and children need to connect with other family members as well. Families can do this in myriad ways, regardless of the geographic distance that separates them. Try to be actively involved with your extended family so traditions can be established or maintained and family wisdom and humor can be passed down through the generations.

"You Go First"

A spouse who is in a low spot in his marriage may feel tempted to say, "I'll show my love and commitment to my spouse after she first proves her commitment to me." This is reminiscent of a grade-school argument. It takes two people to make a marriage work. In the face of difficulties, the first person you should look at to make things better is yourself. As you do that, and make appropriate changes in your own behavior, the low spots will not last as long or be as intense. The secret is that you both "go first."

Dedicated to the One You Love

In this chapter we have emphasized the idea that marriage is a decision. Each of you individually, and then as a couple, decided that you wanted to be married to your sweetheart. The two of you have created a unique relationship. This is the beauty of marriage: that while there are many similarities across marriages, there is also a wonderful distinctiveness to every marriage. Discover the unique ways that you fulfill your marriage commitment as the days, weeks, months, and years go by.

- Pay attention to the ways you communicate with each other verbally and non-verbally.
- Define or describe your communication styles. Use your own words or phrases to describe your communication (for example, "Teddy Bear," "Barely There," and so on).
- What would you say is the "secret ingredient" in your recipe for showing your dedication to your spouse?

Commit yourselves to having the best marriage possible. Remember that you are modeling a marriage as others observe you. Commit to being the best marriage model possible, not because others are watching you, but rather because as you become each other's best spouse, you are the ones who benefit!

CHAPTER 25
Keep Your Marriage Tuned Up

THE KEY: Continually working and playing at keeping your marriage relationship alive and well is a key to a great marriage.

Your marriage is constantly evolving because both of you are continually growing and changing. Many of your interests, tastes, and preferences have stayed the same since you met, but others have changed dramatically. Most people get into ruts in their lives and marriages. To combat this, spouses often need to be reminded of practical suggestions for everyday marriage. Of course, you may already be doing much of what we suggest here, but reminders can help. We have discussed some of the following ideas in greater detail in previous chapters. The key here is for you and your spouse to discuss them regularly so that you create your own ways of keeping your marriage alive.

One of the reasons marriage counseling is so successful with many couples is that the partners commit to a regular time to assess their marriage in detail. Many couples have a relational check-up that goes something like this:

Wife: "So, how do you think our marriage is going?"

Husband: "Why? What have I done that you're not happy with?"

Wife: "Oh, nothing. I just wanted to check in and make sure we are doing okay."

Husband: "I am very happy with our marriage! I love you. How 'bout you?"

Wife: "I think we're doing okay; I'm just wanting to make sure."

We recommend that your relational "exam" be a bit more comprehensive. Take time on a regular basis and check yourselves against the following areas. If you have any questions on a particular section, read the corresponding chapter in this book.

Marriage is a Decision and Commitment.

Commitment to marriage is crucial. Commitment is a decision. Thus, commitment to marriage means that spouses are dedicated to the idea of being married, and married to each other. Couples who are committed to working together to make their marriage work will have a successful and satisfying marriage and will escape the tragedy of divorce.

How is marital commitment measured? Perhaps the simplest way is to look at the effort, time, and attention that you give to your marriage. Happily married couples give adequate time and attention to one another and to their marriage. They find time in their busy lives to do things together. Time together is a priority and is scheduled and planned. Of course, the spouses do not neglect other responsibilities and commitments, but they do not neglect marital time either.

Happily married couples find time to get away together. It doesn't matter if these getaways are overnight stays or longer trips. The point is for the couple to have time together in an activity that is different from their daily routine. The goal is to spend time together and renew their marital relationship, as well as to rest and reflect on the blessings and challenges of life. How often should these getaways occur? That is for individual couples to decide. The frequency of these getaways may vary over the years, but it is important that they occur.

Continually Clarify Expectations and Roles

One of the most crucial areas of discussion and clarification in marriage is expectations and roles. Spouses must ask themselves and each other, "What are my expectations in my role as husband/wife? What are my expectations of my wife/husband?" And, perhaps embedded in these questions are expectations relating to roles: "What do I believe are the roles of a husband or wife, father or mother in marriage?"

Think about your expectations. One way to get a handle on marital expectations for the two of you is to assess just one segment of married life. For example, ask yourself, "What would be my spouse's perfect evening?" Without collaboration, each of you write a description your spouse's view of perfect evening. Then take turns describing to each other what you have written; describe what *you think* your partner's perfect evening would look like. You may be surprised!

Now, discuss with each other what your perfect evening would *really* look like! Have fun and learn from each other as you participate in this discussion. What have you learned from this? We hope one thing you learn is to never take each other for granted. As long as spouses live, and as well as they know each other, they make a mistake if they believe that each knows exactly what the other person expects, wants, or needs.

Continually Develop and Enrich Communication Skills

Most couples employ wonderful strategies that build a foundation for a successful marriage. The first thing that usually happens is that couples develop good communication skills. In fact, most relationships don't go very far if a couple has difficulty communicating. The most frequently reported problem in marriage counseling is poor communication.

The good news is that communication is a skill, and like all skills, it can be improved. So, while good communication is an important first step in building your marriage, it is only the first step on an eternal stairway of improving communication.

I-Messages

Most readers are familiar with "I-messages" or "I-statements" as a means of appropriately communicating feelings and intentions. The following may be a review for you, but it may also add an ingredient that is not present in many I-message techniques. First, remember that the goal of I-messages is to facilitate open, honest, and direct communication. Partners do this by accepting responsibility for and communicating feelings and intentions. A spouse who does not use an I-message can be misinterpreted as complaining and blaming. I-messages have three parts:

1. Describe the *behavior* without blaming.
2. State your *feelings*.
3. State *feared consequences*. (Most I-message communication techniques focus on the first two parts and overlook this third part.)

Thus, using this formula, an appropriate I-message might be "When you are late coming home at night, I feel upset because I think you might have been in an accident." Analyzing that statement, we have, "When you are late coming home at night . . . [describes the *behavior*] . . . I feel anxious . . . [describes your *feelings*] . . . because I think you may have been in an accident . . . [describes the *consequence* that you fear].

This way of speaking conveys feelings and perceptions much more completely than if only the behavior and feelings were stated. In that case, the I-message would have been, "When you are late coming home at night [behavior] I feel upset [feelings]." Such a statement is accurate but incomplete. By adding the feared consequences, the person who was late coming home at night is much less likely to be defensive because he understands his spouse's fear or reason for being upset.

Another example illustrates everyday couple activities in the home: "When you spend evenings scrapbooking, I feel sad because I think you really don't want to interact with me." Such a simple and complete statement communicates in a safe way the feelings of one spouse to the other.

Safety provides structure in communication and other areas of marriage. If using I-statements seems awkward, don't worry about following the technique exactly; rather, take the principles of the technique and integrate them into your personal style.

Show Me That You Heard Me

A different approach that can help to improve communication is captured in the acronym L.U.V. Here, L stands for *listening*, U stands for *understanding*, and V stands for *validating*.

Listening. When you are in the conversation with your spouse, do you really listen to him or her? We convey listening through simple gestures such as making appropriate eye contact and paying attention. Are you reading a newspaper or magazine or watching television? Put down the paper, turn off the television, and pay attention!

Understanding. In conversations with your spouse, do you try to understand him? Understanding is important for both the speaker and the listener. Do you really care what the other person thinks or says? We hope so! Do you really care about how he feels? Do you attempt to understand what the other person is saying? The key is to understand what is being said, not necessarily to agree. Understanding is communicated by simple gestures such as making eye contact, nodding your head in agreement, saying such things as "Uh-huh," "Yes," "OK," or "I understand." It can also be helpful to say something like, "Tell me if I'm getting this right," or, "I heard you say that. . . ." Through these techniques, not only can the listener make sure that she understands, but the speaker can clarify what he is trying to say.

Validating. A listening-and-hearing conversation prepares the participants for the final ingredient in good communication, which is validation. For the speaker, being validated means that she has been listened to and understood. Feeling understood engenders feelings of respect and self-worth. For the listener, validation means a confirmed knowledge of the spouse's feelings, thoughts, or intentions. There is little more important than feeling respected, understood, and validated in conversations with your spouse, particularly in a loving and trusting relationship.

Remember that everyone can improve communication skills. Married couples tend to take each other for granted as the years pass. Pay attention to your communication with your spouse and make it a marital strength.

Solve Problems as They Arise

Another skill that couples develop early in their relationship is the ability to deal with problems. In some ways, the ability to discuss and solve problems together is a subcategory of communication skills. However, it is useful to view problem solving separately.

While we generally think of problem solving as dealing with negative issues, the skill of problem solving also applies to dealing with positive decisions and actions. For example, let's say that a young married couple is approaching the holiday season. His parents have invited the couple to spend the upcoming holiday with them on an all-expenses-paid ocean cruise for a week. Her parents have invited the couple to spend the upcoming holiday with them on an all-expenses-paid trip to Disneyland. Two attractive alternatives! The couple is confronted with the "problem" of deciding how to resolve these generous invitations without offending either family or each other. The couple will engage their best problem-solving skills, including brainstorming possible solutions and looking at all of the options, to determine the best solution and how to implement it. Then the fun begins as they make plans and inform their families of their decision!

Be Flexible—Roll with the Punches

Flexibility—the ability to adapt to the changing nature and demands of marriage—is important in stable and satisfactory marriages. Happily married couples are willing and able to make adjustments in their marriage. As we have discussed, going into marriage, partners often have different expectations about what each will or should do in marriage. Successful couples work as a team and share in the planning and creating of their marital roles and responsibilities. Then, when circumstances change or unexpected events require changing plans, they adapt and help each other out.

For example, if one spouse suddenly becomes very busy with a new time demand—whether from work, extended family needs, or volunteer service—the other spouse may need to shoulder a larger or different portion of the housework or other tasks than originally planned. Couples also need to be flexible in other areas, such as how they manage their finances, how they spend their time socially, and even how they handle their sexual relationship. If both partners are willing to adjust their individual preferences and actions for the benefit of the couple and their marriage, they will have less conflict and greater harmony in their marriage.

Nurture Each Other

We encourage each married couple to have a date night each week. The idea of the weekly date night is that the couple can look forward to and count on those hours together, protected from interference. Once during the week, put your marital relationship first. Except for true emergencies, this weekly date night (or lunch or whatever works for you) needs to be protected from all other interferences. A wife will never believe she is the most important person in her husband's life until he has shown her that he is willing to keep his time commitments to her. The same is true for a husband. Actions speak louder than words.

When researchers asked married couples to define "happy marriage," the straightforward answer they received was that happiness in marriage means feeling respected and cherished. Without exception, couples mentioned the importance of liking and respecting each other and taking pleasure and comfort in each other's company. They expressed the importance of being central in their partner's world and of making their marriage and family the major commitment of their adult life. Partners nurture each other by word and deed. The ways partners speak to, with, and about each other are very important. Of course, respectful language is essential. Also, subtle statements that reinforce the relationship rather than individuals can be important. For example, speak of "our car," "our home," or "our child," rather than "my car," "my home," or "my child."

Have Fun

Having fun and laughing together deepens your relationship. In fact, in a nationwide random phone survey, people rated having fun as a very important ingredient in a happy marriage. The amount of fun that married couples have together emerged as a key factor in their overall marital happiness.

Having fun together is necessary, not optional, for a happy marriage. It is an essential psychological task in keeping a marriage alive and well. To build a successful marriage, couples need "to share laughter and humor and to keep interest alive in the relationship. A good marriage is alternately playful and serious, sometimes flirtations, sometimes difficult and cranky, but always full of life." (Wallerstein and Blakeslee, 1995, p. 332.)

Investing a reasonable amount of time and money for recreation together isn't a luxury, it's a necessity. If you like doing similar things together, having fun is easy. But what if you like to do different things? The answer is to expand your horizons and your interests. Find new activities that you can enjoy doing together. Compromising and taking turns are good ideas and can help you develop new interests. Certainly you did things together before marriage that were mutually enjoyable and sometimes new to one of you, unless one of you was faking it! Continue to do those activities, and discover new ones as well. You don't need to do everything together, but some shared activities are a crucial ingredient of a great marriage.

Be Active in Religious Service, Fellowship, and Worship

Shared religious beliefs and participating actively in a church can be an important anchor for marriage. Worship and church activity may have been an important part of your courtship and dating experiences. They provided opportunities for you to see one another in a religious context, and to join with other people of similar values.

Participation and worship in religious activities gives married couples topics to talk about, values, and shared experiences. Spouses discover a new depth to their relationship and get to know one another in spiritual ways. As a couple worships together, they gain insights into each other's heart and soul that they would not experience otherwise. Also, by being active in a church congregation, a couple can develop significant relationships and friendships. Couples can learn about marriage and parenting in informal conversations, discussions, and interactions, as well as in formal lessons.

Take a Relationship Assessment Inventory

Many couples find useful and fun questionnaires designed specifically to provide information about their relationship. The advantage of these questionnaires is that they organize your responses into scales and charts that compare you with each other in many important areas of marriage. Such information can help you understand your expectations about being married and provide you with great information and ideas to discuss together.

An excellent questionnaire for this purpose is the Relationship Evaluation Inventory (RELATE). RELATE assesses four major areas of marriage: 1) personality characteristics and values; 2) relationship support from family and friends; 3) communication and conflict resolution skills; and 4) family background.

RELATE does not predict whether your marriage will last or tell you if you relationship is good or bad. What RELATE does is give you information so that you and your spouse can clarify and evaluate certain aspects, thoughts, and opinions about your marriage. The unique aspect of RELATE it is that it is designed to be self-administered online and to be interpreted by the couple taking it through the RELATE Report, which you can print after you complete the inventory online.

Partners take RELATE separately online. After both have completed the questionnaire, the computer prepares the 22-page RELATE Report, which organizes information from the inventory responses into scales, graphs, and charts. It provides guidelines and questions to help the couple interpret and understand the report. Information from the RELATE questionnaire doesn't tell couples what to do about their relationship; rather, it gives them information for discussion and planning. RELATE is available on the Internet at www.relate-institute. org. The cost is $20 per couple.

Conclusion

Remember how you found each other and developed a special relationship before your wedding? You had fun together. You learned to trust and to care for each other as you developed your relationship and bonded in social, emotional, spiritual, intellectual, physical, and other ways.

With that foundation, you can feel reassured that even in these days of marriage woes when we hear so much about divorce, you have the power to make your marriage work. Those who are committed to making a marriage last can do so. Viewing marriage as a true partnership is the key. Such a perspective on your marriage will bind you two together in strong emotional and psychological ways. You each have the power you need to make your marriage last as you and your spouse confront and conquer the inevitable difficulties that will occur. Create and live your marital dreams!

Further Reading

The following are some of the many books that we have found to be useful for married couples in an effort to strengthen their marriage.

John Gottman. *Why Marriages Succeed or Fail.* New York: Simon & Schuster, 1994.

Jeffry H. Larson. *The Great Marriage Tune-Up Book.* San Francisco: Jossey-Bass, 2003.

Kevin Leman. *Were You Born for Each Other?* New York: Delacorte, 1991.

Howard J. Markman, Scott M. Stanley, Susan L. Blumberg. *Fighting for Your Marriage: Positive Steps for Preventing Divorce and Preserving a Lasting Love.* San Francisco: Jossey-Bass, 2001.

David H. Olson & Amy K. Olson. *Empowering Couples: Building on Your Strengths.* Minneapolis: Life Innovations, 2000.

Suze Orman. *The Courage to be Rich: Creating a Life of Material and Spiritual Abundance.* New York: Riverhead Books/Putnam, 1999.

Bernard E. Poduska. *Till Debt Do Us Part: Balancing Finances, Feelings, and Family.* Salt Lake City: Shadow Mountain, 2000.

Virginia Satir. *The New Peoplemaking.* Palo Alto, California: Science & Behavior Books, 1988.

Robert F. Stahmann, Wayne R. Young, & Julie G. Grover. *Becoming One: Intimacy in Marriage.* American Fork, Utah: Covenant Communications, Inc., 2004.

John Van Epp. *How to Avoid Marrying a Jerk: The Foolproof Way to Follow Your Heart without Losing Your Mind.* New York: McGraw-Hill, 2006.

Linda J. Waite & Maggie Gallagher. *The Case for Marriage: Why Married People are Happier, Healthier, and Better Off Financially.* New York: Doubleday, 2000.

Judith S. Wallerstein & Sandra Blakeslee. *The Good Marriage: How & Why Love Lasts.* Boston: Houghton Mifflin, 1995.